STATE OF ORIGIN

State of Origin

DAVID OWEN KELLY

PUNCHER & WATTMANN

First published in 2019
Published by Puncher and Wattmann
PO Box 279
Waratah NSW 2298
http://www.puncherandwattmann.com
puncherandwattmann@bigpond.com

National Library of Australia
Cataloguing-in-Publication entry:
ISBN 978-1-925780-43-7
Dewey 362.7234

Cover design by Miranda Douglas
Text design and typesetting by Christine Bruderlin
Printed by Lightning Source

This project has been assisted by the Australian Government through the Australia Council, its arts funding and advisory body.

Australian Government

Australia Council for the Arts

For Jason

Phone Calls

'Murgon . . . ' The woman's answer throws me.

'Hello. This is a long shot. I'm looking for my foster brother, Errol Rebato. His last known place of residence was in Cherbourg, Queensland.'

'You should ring the Cherbourg Police Station.'

'I did ring the Cherbourg Police Station. I was put straight through by Directory Assistance.'

'If there's no one at that station the call comes through to Murgon Police Station.' The woman sighs as if it's a daily mantra. 'We're the next town.'

Murgon. The name sounds like a brand of processed meat.

'Ring Cherbourg tomorrow at lunchtime. Here's another number.'

The woman gives me time to locate a pen and all of a sudden I have the Cherbourg Police Station phone number in front of me, and I'm where I should have been at the beginning.

I thank her. I hang up and my eyes meet those of two ornamental Aboriginal boys I have sitting on the bookshelf next to the photo of Jason and me on holidays. The plaster of Paris boys have been painted with a tan wash, their heads, arms and shoulders made to look as if they're emerging out of the same lump of ochre rock. Both kids are fat-cheeked and broad-nosed with wide expressive mouths. Apart from some photos and other bits and pieces, this ornament is all I have left from our dead mother's estate. It sat on every dressing table in every home our mother lived in since she stepped off the boat from Wales when she was seventeen.

There is no way she could have known that within 12 years of picking her way down the gangplank over the mud-brown Brisbane River she would take ownership of six children, four white and two Aboriginal, but none from her own womb.

Except for a small chip in one of the curls of hair, Mum's plaster of Paris boys have stayed safe in the family. But Mum's two real live Aboriginal boys, Errol and Lindsey, now men in their forties, are missing.

All most people know about Cherbourg is that it's a troubled place which the Aboriginal inhabitants once needed permits to leave. I can't imagine today's inhabitants looking kindly on some white guy walking in willy-nilly asking questions about one of their own. How will I get in? I seem to remember Cherbourg opening a tourist attraction where they had carved emu eggs for sale.

Maybe at an emu farm where visitors are encouraged I could question the employees to see if they know someone called Errol. I'll go in under the cover of tourist. I wonder if Errol would be scared if he had to enter all the gay bars on Oxford Street looking for me. I think he would be. After this I don't feel so bad.

Half an hour later, after a bike ride into Newcastle's city centre, I'm plugged into a different phone, wearing a Madonna-style headset and answering questions people have about their health insurance.

'Welcome to Physician Health Funds. My name is David. How can I help you?'

Nine calls an hour is the target, but calls can range from simple address changes to helping members who have just discovered they need a major operation and want to know if they have the appropriate cover. These latter calls flip the targets out the window. First I ask whether the member has a medical item number, from which I can tell if they are covered for that particular procedure or not. Due to privacy concerns I'm not supposed to be able to tell the nature of the operation, though it's simply a matter of pulling up the Medicare website. The worst part of the job is telling a member that their policy fails to cover the required operation, and if they change their cover to suit then they'll have a year to wait. People cry, rail, and wave figurative fists, but Physician Health has bulletproof glass doors in case they really mean it when they say they are coming to blow us all away.

If the member is thinking of terminating their membership it's my job to remind them of the public hospital waiting lists and the mayhem of an overcrowded public hospital system. Nine times out of 10 the member opts to stay in Physician Health Funds and my job is done. My calls are sometimes taped by my supervisor and played back to highlight the areas where I can improve my customer service. I'm required to hear my own voice – wheedling, adenoidal – building up scenarios of potential disaster.

The only part of working in a call centre that I enjoy is listening to all the background noise in people's homes. The most common sound is their television. I can pick the channel they are watching. Between six and six-thirty the majority watch *The Simpsons*. Then there's the clatter of dinner being made, of china plates being balanced one-handed from cupboards to counter-tops, of the hunt for kitchen implements in the second drawer, and the sounds of hair and lips pressed too close to the receiver. I'm allowed in through a chink in these people's lives. I have their addresses on screen in front of me. I know who visits their psychologist weekly. I know who has a bad back and who has had a vasectomy. I know who takes pills to perform sexually and who has lost a breast to cancer. I can tell who has been committed and who is looking to be, who is separated, and which one got the kids. I could stalk them. The screen in front of me is like an abridged version of their lives. People tell me the most personal things about themselves as if I'm an actual doctor.

'Let's see.' I breathe gently into the black foam ball an inch from my mouth. I apply my fingers to the keyboard as delicately and confidently as a doctor lifting bandages from a patient's wound. For this I earn $22.50 an hour after tax.

At lunchtime the next day I do not ring the Cherbourg police as the operator instructed: Errol, if he's alive, wouldn't want me to tell the police anything. But then it's only because of the police that I've gotten this far. And it's only because of the Royal Commission into Aboriginal Deaths in Custody, which comes up when I search for his name online, that I know Errol was ever in Cherbourg.

I'm running out of time. The average age of mortality for Aboriginal men in Australia is as low as 45. Errol will be 43 in August and Lindsey will be 45 in September. At 4:30pm, while getting ready for work, I change my mind.

It's engaged. I finish dressing and I ring again.

'Murgon.' It's the same woman.

'Hello, I rang yesterday looking for my brother Errol Rebato and you gave me the phone number for Cherbourg?' I say it as a question in case she doesn't remember. 'I've come through to you again.'

'They must be out on patrol. You have to keep trying.'

Her voice now has a smattering of kindness. I flatter myself it's because I'm trying to connect with a lost family member and not ringing for an ambulance or a police car.

'Thanks again.' I decide not to ask the operator personally if she knows anyone called Errol. We both answer phones for a living and I imagine the woman has had the same training in privacy laws.

I should have left for work by now. I start at 5:30pm. Its 4:45 but I'm sure the clock is a little fast. I'll try one more time. The phone rings.

A young man's voice, 'Cherbourg Police.'

'Hi.' *Why did I say hi? I'm not American. I should have met his hello with another hello.* 'Hello, my name's David. This is a shot in the dark. I'm trying to find my foster brother Errol Rebato. I haven't seen him in 20 years.'

Why did I say shot in the dark to a policeman?

'His last known place of residence was in Cherbourg. I don't know what you can tell me due to the privacy laws.' *I'm babbling.* 'When I search for Errol's name online there's a connection between him and the Cherbourg Police Station from the late eighties.'

'You're related?'

Are we related? I could show evidence to this policeman if we were face to face. I could pull out a small blurry photo of Lindsey,

Errol and me at Bullen's African Lion Safari where we'd been taken in the mid-seventies to see Australia's first liger cub, the offspring of a male lion and a female tiger. The sign on the cage said the liger was sterile but would grow much bigger than either of its parents. I remember asking Mum what the word sterile meant.

'Like your father,' Mum said in a vague fashion, as if it wasn't rude.

In the photo we're arranged on top of a log castle. Errol sits between Lindsey and me, staring out, smiling slightly. Lindsey doesn't know what to do with his hands while I'm holding mine out in front of me dangling at the wrists.

'My! Weren't you the little queen of the castle!' is the response when I show friends. I wonder what the policeman would say.

Mum took this photo in the first months after she abandoned Dad for Ron. Lindsey was 13, Errol 12 and I was 11 when we started going on bonding excursions every weekend to 'get to know Ron'. This was before Ron started 'special bondings' with my sister Rayley.

'Yes, I'm his foster brother.' I place the emphasis on the foster word so I can't be charged with misrepresentation. Without actually coming right out and saying it, I want this policeman to understand I'm not Errol's Aboriginal blood brother, that I'm white. I wonder if the policeman is Aboriginal. I've read there are both kinds in Cherbourg, but from his voice I can't pick his colour. I wonder what he thinks of my voice. I have a gay voice.

Neither Lindsey nor Errol knows that Mum is dead.

'Just a minute.' The phone is jammed into the cotton chest of his blue shirt and it sounds like my head is resting against his heart.

I hear him calling out to someone but not getting an answer. He raises the receiver back to his mouth and tells me the person he needs to ask is out the front of the police station and he has to put the phone down. I tell him I'm happy to wait. The receiver clatters against a hard surface and settles.

If I'd rung 20 years ago at this same time in the afternoon and listened through a dropped receiver I could have heard Errol's voice calling out. 'Keep us separated! Or else we'll start fighting again.' I could have heard the two men being put into different cells. If I'd stayed listening I could have heard the sound of one man sleeping and the other man dying. I would have been able to hear the commotion of discovery. But that was 20 years ago when I was unable to hear anything beyond the disco beats of Oxford Street.

'Are you there?'

'Yes.'

'Yeah, he's left Cherbourg. He's on his way to Brisbane.'

He states it as if he's just glimpsed Errol growling past the police station. As if he could have yelled out 'Stop! Stop! There's a man on the phone. He's got a gay voice. He says he's your brother.'

Sunlight splinters off the windscreen of a red Monaro. I can't see the driver's face, but he's got black hair. A hand with a big silver ring taps out a drumbeat on the door panel. It's Errol. He hits the accelerator and fishtails out of there. My brother is alive and speeding to Brisbane.

'Thank you,' I say, like a robot.

I hang up.

Everything has turned two-dimensional as if I'm suffering sunstroke. The ornamental boys look small and unnecessary.

'My brother is alive,' I whisper to them.

I close the window and whisper into the curtains. 'My brother is alive.'

I close the back door and hear the click. 'My brother is alive.'

I unlock my bike and wheel it to the footpath, saying it, tasting the words.

In time with my feet pumping the bike pedals down the street, I yell over and over again, the wind tossing the words over my shoulder. 'My brother is alive. My brother is alive.'

Extract from the Royal Commission into Aboriginal Deaths in Custody: Report of the Inquiry into the Death of Mitchell Pringle

In mid-June 1987 Mitchell returned to Cherbourg to attend a funeral for a friend who had died of a heart attack in Brisbane Prison a few days before.

Mitchell's cousin, Chloe, and her boyfriend, Errol Rebato, also travelled to Cherbourg for the funeral and remained there. Mitchell and Errol had first met some three years earlier at Musgrave Park. Although they were not close friends they saw each other occasionally when Errol began courting Chloe.

At about 7.00 am or 8.00am on 9 July 1987, Mitchell went to a friend's house in Barber Street, Cherbourg and began to drink moselle from a cask. Towards the middle of the morning Mitchell and some other friends travelled to Murgon and purchased two more casks of moselle and some beer. When they returned, they were joined by other friends. The group headed to a place near the Cherbourg sewerage works known as Goona Gully.

On their way to Goona Gully, Mitchell and his group called on his cousin, Chloe, and invited her to come drinking. Errol was opposed to this, as he did not want her to drink. Despite Errol's protestations, Chloe went with Mitchell. Errol remained behind at the house where they were staying.

Mitchell's group all became very intoxicated.

Ultimately they decided to go to the canteen. On the way they passed Errol Rebato who had also been drinking and by this time was intoxicated. When Errol saw Chloe he again tried to persuade her not to go drinking with Mitchell ... Soon a fight broke out between the two men.

At about 3.00 pm, Senior Sergeant Miles and Constable Best of the Cherbourg Aboriginal police were on a routine patrol in the police van when they saw the two fighting in Jerome Street. Miles alighted and approached the two young men. According to the police, Mitchell appeared to be the more intoxicated of the two. Miles warned them to stop fighting and to go home. Errol, according to Miles 'just took it, but the other fellow, Mitchell, kept on wanting to fight ...' Following the warning Mitchell and Errol parted and walked away in opposite directions. Mitchell shouted that Errol had started the fight and that he would 'get him' the next day. Once the situation was apparently defused, the police left and resumed their patrol.

The changeover in police shifts occurred at 4.00 pm. Best drove Miles to the police station then continued on to pick up Constable Parsons and Constable Fielding. Fielding was Mitchell's cousin and had been an Aboriginal policeman for 11 years. Best told Parsons and Fielding about the altercations between the two young men. Best then returned to his home which was next door to the watch-house.

Parsons and Fielding began patrolling the Cherbourg area and at about 4.20 pm they saw Mitchell and Errol shaping up to each other in the backyard of a house between Broadway and Barber Streets.

The police stopped their vehicle, alighted and walked over ... Fielding considered that Mitchell was the more intoxicated and aggressive of the two. The police saw that Mitchell had a cut and swollen lip which was bleeding a little.

Both of the young men were arrested for disorderly conduct ... Fielding took hold of Mitchell while Parsons took hold of Errol. Both went quietly and got into the van without incident.

The police drove their two prisoners to the watch-house, which was a short distance away and about 100 metres from the police station. Across the road and about 50 metres away was the home of the watch-house keeper, who at the time was Best.

Mitchell and Errol alighted from the van and walked quietly to the charge counter in the watch-house.

The police instructed the two prisoners to remove their belts, shoes, socks and shirts.

At 4.45 pm Errol was placed in cell No. 1 by Fielding, and Mitchell was placed in cell No. 3 by Parsons. The two were separated by cell No. 2 and were out of reach and sight of each other.

A crucial exchange occurred between Mitchell and Best. Best asked Mitchell to remove his socks, Mitchell complained that it was cold and said, 'What, do you think I'll hang myself with them?' Errol had difficulty recalling but thought that Mitchell may have been complaining about the cold and talking about his socks. It was a cold afternoon in Cherbourg and Mitchell was allowed to keep his socks. Both were given blankets.

Parsons said that when he locked Mitchell in his cell 'he seemed alright' apart from being drunk. Once Errol was locked into his cell he went to sleep. Fielding and Parsons then drove the short distance to the police station. Parsons recorded the charge in the watch-house charge book. They then resumed their patrol of Cherbourg.

Errol and Mitchell were the only two people at the watch-house. There were no other prisoners and no watch-house keeper or other officer stationed on duty at the watch-house at the time.

At about 5.00 pm Best walked from his residence to the watch-house in order to see how many meals would be required for prisoners. He approached the outside enclosure of the watch-house. He noticed Mitchell seated on the edge of the bunk with his feet on the floor and was alarmed to see that there was a football sock around his neck. The other end of the sock had been passed through the bars and was tied to the wire grille ceiling just outside the cell. Mitchell's hands were hanging limply. Best looked in at Errol two cells away and could see he was sleeping.

Best ran back to his residence and called Fielding and Parsons on the two-way radio asking them to hurry back to the watch-house. Best did not go into the cell because he was frightened and concerned to have witnesses with him. He was unable to ring the hospital, as there was no telephone at his house.

As soon as Fielding and Parsons received the radio message they returned to the watch-house where they saw Best waiting at the front. Best told them that Mitchell was hanging in the cell.

The police rushed to Mitchell's cell. Fielding held him under his arms while Parsons lifted his feet and undid the socks from the wire grille and from around his neck. Fielding and Parsons then laid the body on the bed. Parsons checked for a pulse and other signs of life, but was unable to detect any. As the Aboriginal police had no training in resuscitation techniques, none were undertaken. Instead, Best rushed to the hospital and returned with a doctor. The doctor examined the deceased, found no signs of life and pronounced life extinct.

On My Eighth Birthday

There are four types of trips we take north across the Brisbane River:

- pick up a baby for adoption
- take delivery of a child for fostering
- visit the Queensland museum
- go to the Brisbane exhibition grounds for the annual show called the EKKA.

Otherwise we stay south-side.

For Karen, Beth and me, the three adopted, there is no remembered 'before' our north side pick-ups. No memories of mothers' smiling faces leaning down and tucking us in – it didn't happen. We draw blanks when we try to remember who our real parents are. We were newborns. The upshot of this is we can while away hours and hours imagining the true identities of our real mothers and fathers. But this has to be done in secret so our adopted Mum and Dad won't get upset and think we don't love them.

The fostered, on the other hand, have real memories. Lindsey, if he can be bribed, tells a story of holding onto his mother's hand

and being chased through the bush by something that catches them and pulls him from her and he never sees his mother again. Until he saw the policemen, he says he thought the things chasing them were lions.

On my eighth birthday, after the hip hip hoorays, and the traditional birthday story of how as a newborn I had hair the colour of pumpkin, Mum's hand stops mid-slice through my birthday cake. She says she has something important to tell me.

'About the woman who gave you that orange-coloured mop.' Mum's eyes are filled with gifts. 'Your birth mother.'

My body turns to fizz.

'Molly?' Dad warns. 'Are you sure he's not too young?'

Mum regards Dad for two seconds and then he's dismissed.

'I know her real name and one other thing.'

My mind turns to fizz.

'Now don't get too excited,' Mum warns, sliding the first slice of cake in front of me, 'because I will tell you all the details when you turn eighteen. When you're old enough.'

The fizz is gone.

It takes all of my concentration to reach out and lever up a spoonful of cake.

'What if you forget?' I ask, pretending not to care.

'I won't forget,' she replies. She plates cake slices for my spell-bound brothers and sisters. 'I've written it down.'

I can't maintain the act. She is telling me to wait 10 years. The cake in my mouth turns to grit.

I once saw a movie about a beautiful, evil queen who chokes to death on the sand that's filling up her dead husband's pyramid. So awful was her death that I went to the library and borrowed books on ancient Egypt to find out if the story was true. I still don't exactly know, but all of a sudden I can't breathe.

'That's not fair!' I yell, shucking off my chair.

'Molly.' Dad throws up his hands and leaves the table. 'Now see what you've done!'

'And this is why I'm not going to tell you, David,' Mum says, ignoring him. 'You're not old enough and you've become hysterical.'

'But why did you say anything?'

'I wish I hadn't, but this would have been your birth mother's job to cut your birthday cake. She must be feeling terrible right now.'

'Please tell me a little bit more. Please? Please?'

'One thing. That's all. Just one thing and then you must not ask me until you're eighteen. Okay?'

'Okay.'

'The nurses, when they handed you over, said that there was something interesting, something out of the ordinary about your birth.'

Without Mum having to say another word, it's obvious.

I'm the son of a movie star.

I can't wait 10 years. I need to know now. While Mum does the dishes and Dad relaxes on the couch, I stretch up my arms and fake a yawn. I amble out of Mum's field of vision and wander down the carpet runner. Lindsey is the only one watching.

Two bedside cabinets stand like sentries on either side of the double bed. Mum's side is closest to the door.

Like a trainer putting his arm into the mouth of a circus lion, I slip my forearm into the open bottom drawer and start to feel for paper objects, expecting at any moment for my hand to scrape against rough tongue.

'What do you think you are doing?' Mum's voice freezes the room.

'Looking for . . . my birth mother.'

'I'm your mother!' The muscles in her face twitch. 'She gave you up!' She grabs my arm and pulls me from the floor. 'Do you hear me? (WHACK) If I ever find you going through my things again you'll get a thrashing you won't forget. Now get to your room.'

She pushes me out, slams the door and storms to the kitchen. Despite the humiliation of being smacked on my birthday I can't stop thinking the information belongs to me.

I will have to discover it another way, a secret way.

If I'm the child of a movie star, a movie star had to have come to Australia.

I'll have to find someone to ask, an adult who won't get suspicious and alert Mum.

Fertility

There is a ritual we perform in the call centre when the call volume is low. One of the supervisors takes off her wedding band and ties string around it, and all the new employees who haven't been tested line up in a row. I am her plant. The aim of the ritual is to predict the gender of a person's first born. They all line up with one flat palm outstretched – the newly married, the single girls whose only pictures above their workstations are of dogs, cats and horses, and the women who spend a fortune on IVF. If the future child is a girl the ring is supposed to go round and round in a circle over the palm. If it's a boy it swings back and forth across the palm in a line. Men from middle management warily watch us from the sidelines and scoff – until I'm called forward to demonstrate. The ring hangs dead over my open hand.

I've never wanted kids but this still doesn't excuse why I let myself be used like this. I could stomp off declaring gays are more than capable of having children. I think I act like this to set people up. Something in me has a habit of looking for the worst. I use homophobia to set a trap for homophobia: the reverse of the Queensland police who once upon a time sent undercover officers into public toilets to entrap homosexuals. Unlike them I don't make any arrests. I keep the findings to myself as if compiling dossiers.

Who is Your Favourite Movie Star?

We're not allowed to talk to strangers. That is Mum's number one rule. The Beaumont children were snatched off a beach talking to strangers. I have to break this rule. At the State Emergency Service barbecue Mum and Dad are hosting in the backyard, I stand beside the esky handing out cold beer.

'Do you know any movie stars that came to Australia?' I whisper to any grown-up who comes into earshot. I soon discover men don't have favourite movie stars. I can hear Mum laughing her tinkling laugh with Dad's dark and handsome best friend, Ron. Soon the whole party is drunk and no one takes me seriously.

The next day I ask the old man who lives next door. 'Do you know any movie stars that came to Australia?'

'Let me see,' he says, stretching his long sinewy arm along the rake handle. 'Oh, yes, an A-Grade movie star. Ava Gardner.'

'Was it in 1965?' I whisper.

'Yes, it could have been. It was *On the Beach*. She was one of the most beautiful of all time.'

All I hear him say was it could have been and this is enough. I hide the library book about movie stars under my mattress.

Women in tight clothes lie like cats on rugs, or hug red satin cushions to their chests. The men slump in armchairs smoking, or lean against doorways in bad moods.

And then there she is.

Beautiful and strong-looking, with a cleft in her chin like a man's. But she scares me. She hasn't got freckles and pumpkin-coloured hair. She looks like she has claws.

I call an emergency tree meeting.

Each kid has their own tree in the backyard.

'I know who my real mother is. Her name is Ava Gardner. She is a movie star.'

I open the book to the photo.

'This is my mother. In real life her hair is a lot more orangey than that.'

The three of them look at her for the longest moment. No one says anything.

'She came to Australia and made a movie but had to give me up because she was so busy.'

'You're a liar,' Lindsey says quietly. He turns to climb down out of the tree. 'You look nothing like her.'

I am Royal

Did anyone survive the terrible murder of the Russian Royal family?

Olden time people in a carriage pulled by horses race across the television screen. Then five children run across lawn in front of a palace.

Like old thunder, heavy music deep from the throats of men rolls out over the appearance of their names.

Olga Tatiana Maria Anastasia Alexei

One after another their faces swim forward. Despite the pictures being black and white I know they all must have orangey hair.

Did any of the Princesses survive that day in the cellar of Ipatiev House?

A prickling sensation takes hold of my scalp and spine. None of the others are interested in the program. Lindsey's attention is buried in the guts and glue of his plastic aeroplane, while Beth and Karen are colouring in.

Through the kitchen doorway Mum is preoccupied with rolling out pie pastry. Everyone is completely unaware of the revelations unfolding before me.

Anastasia was seventeen when the soldiers of the Russian Revolution ushered the Royal family into the cellar with the intent of murdering them all. Rumours persist that a fortune in diamonds and other precious gems, sewn into the hems of their clothes, and hidden in their corsets, helped deflect the bullets, and somehow one of the Royal Princesses survived. That Princess Anastasia escaped.

At the library I swap books of movie stars for ones about the Russian Royal family.

The faces of my real family stare back at me. The photos are all black and white. There is one of the five children with just their shaved heads. I can't tell who's who. I'm surprised because the picture can only mean head lice.

If I didn't have hair no one could tell I wasn't one of them. Not even Lindsey.

This book is my family's photo album.

I lock the bathroom door and prop the open book behind the taps. Their shaved heads stare back saying, *what are you waiting for?* I pull my hair away from my face. It's the same delicate skull. The scissors are kept in the bathroom drawer. Soldiers are knocking on the door. Raising the open blades to the side of my head I hack off clumps of hair and let them fall.

Princess Anastasia escaped the murder of our family and met a nice soldier from the White Army. Running and hiding, running and hiding, Anastasia later gave birth to this man's daughter, and then, always running and hiding, Anastasia's daughter grew up. Another nice man helped them to run and hide. They came to Brisbane where she gave birth to me. But the assassins discovered where they were and she had to give me up, for my own safety.

'Open this door at once! Do you hear me? We do not lock doors in this house!'

The beating on the door becomes louder.

My birth mother had to leave me behind.

Mum shoves the door open. Lindsey, Karen and Beth are straining to get a good look.

'What have you done?' Mum yells.

'I just wanted to see what it would look like.'

'You stupid boy! You've got school tomorrow!'

Mum snatches Dad's hair clippers from the cupboard.

'You are getting sillier by the day!' she says. 'And you're spending far too much time looking in the mirror.'

Blood

'What's this word?'

The man next door comes to the fence. He takes the book from my hands.

'Haemophilia?' He turns it over and reads out the title: '*The Romanovs.*'

'Wow,' he presents the photo of five shaved heads to me, 'these kids look like you with your new haircut!'

'I think they had nits.' I realise he must think I had the same affliction. 'I don't have nits. I cut my own hair to see what it would look like and Mum had to fix it!'

'Really? It says here that two of the five lost their hair due to measles and the other three shaved their heads in sympathy.'

'They're all really nice,' I say, like I've had the pleasure of their company. 'What does haemophilia mean?'

'Oh, the Romanovs were cursed by it. It's a disease that means if you hurt yourself, even just a tiny bit, you can bleed to death just like that!' The old man clicks his fingers. 'Down through the generations it's passed, from the mother to the boy child if I remember correctly. Girls don't get it.'

'I could die?' I shriek, remembering the scissor blades against my skull.

I wheel away from the fence. I find Beth and tell her I'm calling an emergency tree meeting, that I'm in mortal danger, that even a paper cut . . .

I strip an old sheet into ribbons, which I wrap about each limb.

Once again Lindsey, Karen and Beth assemble in my tree's lower branches. I announce I've found my true family at a terrible price.

'Not again,' Beth whispers.

'This is true, and I've got the pictures to prove it.'

Lindsey takes the book. I put both my hands against my shaved head.

'Look at me,' I say. 'And then look at them. I'm Royal, but if I hurt myself I might die. It's a disease that has cursed my entire family.'

Lindsey looks at the line of four bald princesses and one bald prince.

'They look like they had the nits!' He turns the book and shows the girls. They snort.

'You idiots! They had the measles.'

Lindsey flicks through the pages. I can tell he is trying to find reasons why it's not true.

'My family were all supposed to be killed by soldiers, but Princess Anastasia escaped and met a nice man who helped her and they had a daughter who grew up and looked after her. Then that daughter met a nice man and had a baby and that baby was me.'

'But why did they give you away?' There is now a hint of triumph in Lindsey's voice.

'Because soldiers were after them and she couldn't carry me.'

I can see Lindsey calculating my story and reliving his one memory of being chased through the bush in his mother's arms, of being caught and ripped away. He can't deny what happened to my family because of what happened to him.

'I guess it could be true,' he says, lowering himself to the ground with his eyes hidden. 'But that doesn't mean you're king of me!'

Grave

I don't have a designated workspace so at the start of each shift I have to scour the call centre for an empty desk. I steer clear of the desks decorated with photos of smiling children. I learnt my lesson after a photo of one went missing from a desk where I'd sat after the last ring swinging ritual. The mother, who'd nodded enthusiastically at the sight of the ring hanging dead over my palm, asked me accusingly, three times, if I'd taken it – as if, because I can't have any, I'd want her fat brat. I said no once, twice, then gave up. Now I sit at the vacated desks of the childless, the ones decorated with laminated cards heralding sayings like 'If you want the rainbow you've got to put up with the rain.'

My favourite saying is cradled in ornate curlicues:

Life is not measured by the number of breaths we take, but by the moments that take our breath away.

I can't imagine any of these cards going missing.

One of the biggest mass graves in Australia is located in the grounds of Newcastle's Christchurch Cathedral. No one exactly knows where it is: there's been a mass forgetting. The city itself is complicit with putting all those people underground. It watched them die.

In 1866, during a violent July storm, the SS *Cawarra* tried to enter the harbour mouth. The citizens, alerted by alarms set off at the lighthouse, lined up to see if she would make it. The ship had her back broken on the oyster bank and was soon awash in huge waves. It was mid-morning. The majority of the men whose job it was to row the rescue craft were drunk. All but one of sixty-two people perished. The bodies were all buried in one grave.

In the 1980s, when Council workers repaired a retaining wall at the edge of the Cathedral's grounds, bones spilled out onto the footpath. The workers shoved them back into the holes and moved on.

If you walk out along the northern break-wall of the harbour and stop at the right spot, you get the same viewpoint of Newcastle as the people who clambered up into the rigging to wait for the rescue that never came.

Bad things have happened everywhere, and I can't shake the feeling that Queensland, the earth and air of the place, is to blame for the rotten things that happened in my family.

Queensland

On the trip to get Errol we were also supposed to take possession of a girl called Sasha, Lindsey and Errol's blood sister. But the journey to get them has been delayed because Dad had to finish enclosing the side verandah and converting the space into two new bedrooms. One for one of the girls, and the other for a second paying boarder we are taking in to help feed and clothe us all. We already have one boarder, a farm girl who needs to be close to town to attend high school. Her name is Alison and she boards in the bedroom closest to the bathroom for sixteen dollars a week.

According to Mum, Dad was too slow renovating the old verandah, and in the meantime another family came and took Sasha. Mum was really upset because she wanted to keep the three siblings together. She accused Dad of dragging his tools because she thought he didn't want to get two at once.

If you're to believe Mum, the reason for all their adopting and fostering was because Dad married Mum without telling her he couldn't have children. Instead of divorce Mum punished him with a nearly instant brood of six, and no government agency was there to say 'Whoa, hold your horses. Perhaps try counselling.'

I'm an old hand at those journeys north-side, and by the time we went to get Errol I had long since discovered that being the keeper of family history was an important role, and one that could be turned to my own advantage.

'Here it comes!' I say. 'It's over the next hill!'

And as soon as the collection of small, pale green migrant houses appears, angled down the side of a wooded hill to the railway line, the words spill out.

'Look Mum! Your first proper home in Australia!' And then in tandem, because we both know she will say it:

'The size of a shoebox!'

And then both of us laughing at the memory of it, laughing as if we were both glad to be out of there, and Lindsey's eyes narrowing as if he's tallying up numbers, and Karen and Beth's look of bewilderment, not realising the power I am taking by inserting myself in my mother's story and leaving them all out.

Lindsey is silent for the bulk of these trips. It is only when he can see the police horses stamping and shaking their manes in the grounds of the Queensland Police Academy that he states quietly how when he is older he is going to arrest people who lie and do bad things. He doesn't say it to anyone in particular, but I take it as a personal threat.

The signal for Mum to start rolling Dad's first cigarette on the journey occurs when the car drives past the tobacco farm.

'Mum,' I say, leaning eagerly forward, 'Dad's cigarette?'

Mum clicks her tongue and whacks her own forehead to make us all laugh. She takes the tobacco pouch from the glove box, opens it and retrieves the envelope of papers. Pulling two free, she licks one and sticks the wet edge to the dry edge of the other, making a miniature white double bed like hers and Dad's. Dipping her fingers back into the pouch she lifts out clumps and hanging tendrils of tobacco, deposits them down the middle of the white paper bed, and presses them together into one long thin tobacco figure.

Dad watches her from the corner of his eye. I love the way he watches her, and the way she knows she is being watched. Once she is finished with the figure in the bed she lets it lie there for a moment and then starts to roll him backwards and forwards between her forefingers and thumbs, backwards and forwards, backwards and forwards. Watching these actions makes me want to be the one who is being watched. Mum raises the cocoon of tobacco to her lips like a tiny harmonica and licks along the edge. Then she runs it up and down between her fingers checking for bumps. Mum doesn't smoke but she always puts it in her mouth and lights it with Dad's heavy cigarette lighter. After two drags she leans over and places the cigarette between his lips.

Lindsey only went on one fewer trip than me, but instead of fighting for his position in the family as I did for mine, he let circumstances wash over him. When we went to get Beth, I think Lindsey stopped holding his breath and started to drown under the tidal wave of siblings. I think I fought for proximity to our mother because, despite the fact I fantasised about my birth mother, I couldn't bear the thought of losing the only one I'd ever known. Lindsey had already lived through the experience of being taken from his real mother and because he is a foster child he knows he can't rely on it never happening again. Unlike the process of adoption, which is permanent, fostering can be temporary.

Royal Visit

Thirty minutes after crossing the Brisbane River, Dad's Holden passes through the orphanage gates and pulls to a stop. Everyone tumbles out. Karen and Beth start a game of chase round a collection of tall trees, stirring up a cloud of insects. I stumble out and throw up onto the gravel.

'He's carsick,' my mother calls. I look up to see a nun standing watching from the top of the main building's stairs. Beside her is a boy with wavy black hair and pale brown skin. He looks uncertain.

'Bees!' Karen and Beth yell, running back, slapping their arms and jumping into the car. I don't know how a bee sting would affect my haemophilia and I don't want to die in a place full of potential replacements so I fling myself back inside. I scream to wind up the windows, and as the glass rises in front of our eyes I see the boy at the top of the stairs break into laughter.

'Don't panic,' the nun calls. 'They don't sting. They're harmless. They're native bees.'

I am embarrassed by my panic, and amazed I've never heard of bees that don't sting. The boy at the top of the steps is still smiling, at my expense, and I realise I'm not car sick, I'm sick because of him.

The nun is reaching out her hands and beckoning us.

The three of us quietly get out of the car. Mum and Dad strike out across the gravel towards the nun but Lindsey turns in the other direction. Veering sideways with his arms stretched right out Lindsey lets the moving cloud roll right over him. He looks like something trapped in the static of a cold television screen. The bees don't attack. The nun isn't lying.

Dad greets the nun at the top of the stone stairs and everyone is introduced to Errol.

'Where's Lindsey?' Mum asks.

'In the bees,' Beth says, and everyone turns to see Lindsey standing with his eyes closed concentrating on the feeling of insects bunting into his skin.

'Lindsey!' Dad calls out, 'get out of those insects and come and meet your new brother.'

'I'm not new,' Errol says lightly.

'Of course not, darling!' Mum bends down to him. 'Lindsey's already your brother, and I hope it doesn't take too long for you to feel like we're your real family as well.'

'Amen,' the nun says, with a slight bow.

Lindsey moves slowly across the ground and, like a crippled robot, levers each leg up the stone stairs. Dad makes an exasperated noise and pulls him the rest of the way by the arm and lines him up face to face with Errol.

'He's shy,' Mum says.

'Errol, this is Lindsey.' Dad has a hold of both their arms as if he's staging a conversation between sock puppets. 'Lindsey, this is Errol.'

Lindsey inclines his head and Errol nods quickly back.

'There's a bee in your hair,' Errol says, pointing to the curls above Lindsey's right ear.

Lindsey tries to twist away before Dad can cuff the insect but he is too late. Karen lets fly a squeal.

'It's not dead but it doesn't look very well,' Beth says, matter-of-factly.

'Come inside, come inside,' the nun says.

As we move forward, Lindsey drops down in a protective huddle over the bee. He turns and runs down the stairs towards the tree where the bees have their hive. He is whispering into his cupped hand.

The room we've entered doesn't have much furniture. Silent children wearing small smiles stand about in groups of threes and fours. We walk through them into a dormitory where identically made up beds, narrow and thin, are aligned down each wall.

Errol goes to one of the beds and lifts a little case from the floor. With his head held high he hurries through the door without look-ing back.

'Looks like the little blighter can't get away quick enough!' Dad says.

'We do what we can,' the nun says simply, and this time I know she is lying.

As we leave the building with Errol leading the way, all the other orphans stand at the windows waving.

'Careful, Errol!' Karen warns, as we get to the car. 'Don't stand in David's spew.'

Some of the children start to wave coloured items of clothing at us through the orphanage windows and I imagine they're flags and we're the Romanovs and we are so pleased with what we've seen on our orphanage inspection we are taking one of them with us. I wave graciously back. I am Alexei Romanov and Dad is the Tsar Nicholas and Mum the Tsarina.

'Goodbye, Errol! Have a nice trip!'

The voices of the children left behind take on a desperate edge. They entreat us to enjoy the drive home, the day, the year and our lives: anything to stop our car turning out onto the road and driving away without them.

'COME BACK SOON!'

Dad hits the accelerator. The windows are rolled down and hot air buffets our heads. Mum looks exhausted. Halfway home I give in and sneak a peek at Errol. He catches me looking and smiles. The smile isn't too shy and isn't a grin.

Lindsey is sitting with his eyes closed feeling the wind on his face.

Tree Giving

Several days after Errol's arrival we hold a meeting under the clothesline. The first reason for the meeting is to impress upon him that he can't just walk in and take whatever he wants. We each have our own tree. The coffee is Beth's, the umbrella is Karen's, Lindsey has the loquat, and I have the corner privet close to the garage. After he agrees never to climb anyone else's tree uninvited, we all shake hands. He is then granted the tree in the far right-hand corner of the yard with waterviews of the back-neighbour's swimming pool. It's explained that neither Mum nor Dad must ever hear us talking about our real parents as this would upset them greatly. After he promises never to say a word, I reveal he is living with a real prince and tell him my terrible story. Then he's invited to play the Romanov game.

Lindsey, who is always Captain of the assassins, shows him how to use old fence palings for swords and rifles to kill us. The girls show him how they pretend to sew jewels into the hems of their clothing, and how they flail about as the bullets bounce off their bodies. I show him how Anastasia always stumbles away to freedom, and how, as the Prince with haemophilia, I die by bayonet.

We play one round of the Romanovs and then Errol is told he must hold his first tree meeting and tell us where he has come from. I'm not expecting anything exciting — Lindsey's one story is flat and dull and he doesn't like telling it. At the base of Errol's tree he decides he's not coming, and walks off to his own.

Errol's stories are wild and untamed. He starts making noises of birds flying above him. He makes swimming movements with his hands for the fish that used to swim around him. His teeth flash and his eyes laugh. He rocks backwards and forwards. The tree sways dangerously. Karen has wedged herself into the lowest, safest fork; but Beth is riding her branch like it's a bucking bronco. A song bursts out of Errol's mouth in a woman's voice and he claps his hands in a slow rhythm.

Through the waving foliage I see Lindsey climb down out of his tree as if he's being pulled by an invisible thread. He halts at the edge of Errol's tree. His eyes are closed and his face is turned towards his brother. His mouth is open to the sky. He is feeding on Errol's sounds: wind, chickens, a dog barking. Errol's mouth is a speaker box dialled to the past.

'Lindsey!' The woman's voice is coming out of Errol's mouth. Errol is hugging himself, rocking. 'Come here you little rascal, where have you been?'

'There, there. Don't cry, Lindsey. Don't cry. You're all right. You're here now. There, there.'

Thick cords of water are running down Lindsey's face. His shirt is soaking wet. His eyes are focused on something a million miles away and his hands and jaw work woodenly like a puppet's. He senses me staring. He shakes his head and snarls, rakes the tears with his knuckles and launches himself into the tree. He scrambles past the three of us like a drowning man trying to reach the surface and seizes Errol by the throat:

'Stop. STOP!'

Rayley

After we miss out on Sasha, Mum is determined to get a foster girl and that's when we get Rayley. Rayley is older than Karen by one year and with her arrival she becomes the oldest girl.

In a quiet tree giving ceremony, the unclimbable pawpaw is given to her and we neglect to inform her of the symbolic first tree meeting, because we already know her stories off by heart.

The reason Rayley had been put into a children's home is her real mother didn't want her anymore. Rayley had been minding her little brother and he'd fallen out of a front-yard tree and died impaled on a fence spike. Rayley's mother blamed her. Or so Rayley kept saying.

Rayley's stories never stop and have become real rivals to mine. Karen and Beth are enthralled. I can hear them oohhing and aah-hing on the blanket Rayley spreads out at the foot of her pawpaw. Before our family Rayley has been in four others, or so she says, and she has seen lots of things like a little dog dying after protecting her from a brown snake.

Since Rayley started telling her stories Karen and Beth have lost interest in playing the Romanovs. From my tree I can see the three girls start to make up a game called Brown Snake.

'Don't listen,' I say, swinging down. 'Her stories can't be true.'

And when she keeps speaking . . . 'Liar, liar, liar, liar.'

Before long, Rayley's stories are dismissed before they are out of her mouth. I get my sisters back. I reward them with paper cut-out crowns I've made and coloured in. There is a presentation ceremony where I, King of Diamonds, crown Karen, the Grand Duchess of Emeralds, and Beth, the Grand Duchess of Rubies.

Rayley begs to play and I am merciful. I make her the Grand Duchess of Opals because Opals are unlucky (but I don't tell her that).

I can understand Rayley's mother not wanting her. I don't want her. But the situation with Lindsey, Errol, and Sasha, their sister we nearly got, is different. Three unwanted from the same family – how is it possible?

When I ask Mum she explains the government has decided that Lindsey and Errol's parents couldn't look after them properly. She says this is rubbish, and that the government is wrong.

*

The three of us boys sleep in the back sleep-out. Lindsey and Errol have bunk beds and I've been moved to a single. Rayley and Beth have the front room and Karen is given one of the new rooms all to herself. In any other family the new room would have been given to the oldest girl but Rayley is only new and this wouldn't be fair. The new boarder has the other new bedroom and Mum and Dad sleep in the main bedroom. Mum announces she's decided that the house is full. No more kids. We all breathe a sigh of relief.

1st diagram of sleeping arrangements:

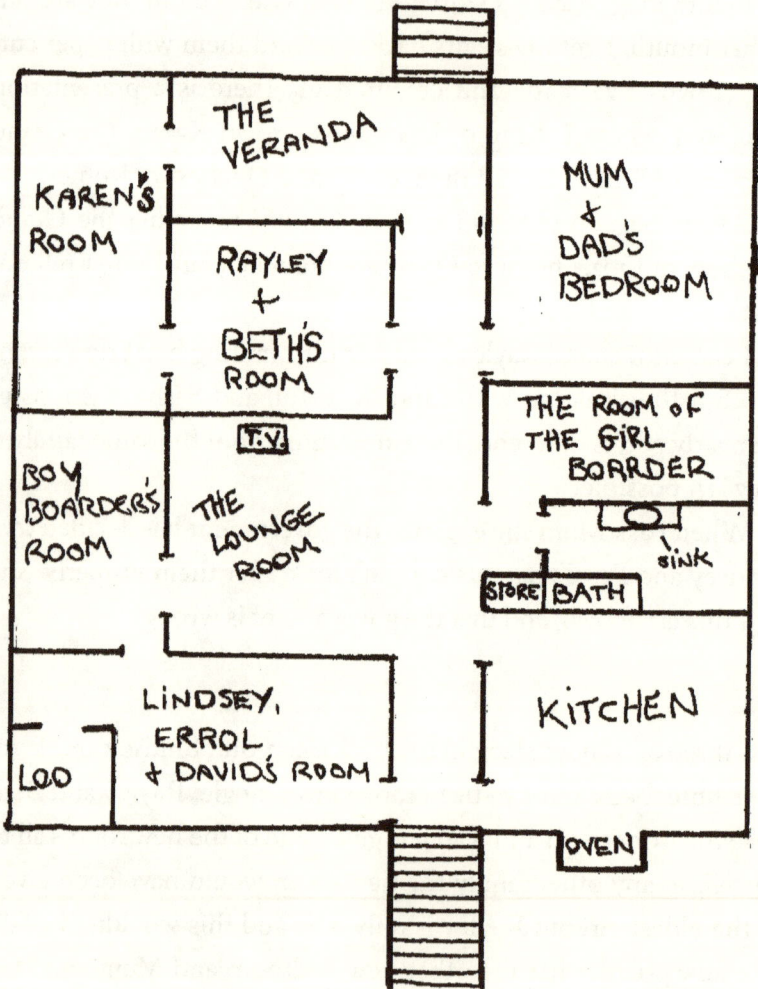

A Room of One's Own

Errol has bronchiolitis. Every morning and night, on doctor's advice, Mum has to beat his back with cupped hands till he spits phlegm from his lungs into a bucket.

The beating of Errol's back is a nightly attraction. The girls and I sit on the floor in front of the couch. Errol lies over Mum's knees like a travel blanket. Errol cries at the beginning of each back beating, and Mum cries softly along with him. From my position on the floor she looks like a saint. If I squint, I can see my Great Grandmother, the Empress Alexandra in her Red Cross nursing uniform tending to sick and wounded Russian soldiers. I decide to be a doctor or a nurse when I grow up.

Lindsey watches from behind the couch. He watches Mum fall in love with Errol because he is being so brave.

Unlike Lindsey, I'm reasonably sure of where I stand in Mum's heart. I am the first child picked up and have had more time to make an imprint. I am also white in the way she is white and no one can tell I'm not her real son. No one asks her at the shops, 'Where did you get him?'

In order of appearance we descend like this:

- David (me): adopted
- Lindsey: fostered
- Karen: adopted
- Beth: adopted
- Errol: fostered
- Rayley: fostered.

In order of age, we descend like this:

- Lindsey
- Errol
- David (me)
- Rayley
- Karen
- Beth.

The male boarder finishes high school and moves out, and Mum and Dad decide the family can survive without replacing him, so one of us boys is going to get the empty bedroom. Errol isn't in the race because he just got here. Lindsey and I assail Mum and Dad from all sides. The bin never needs emptying or the animals feeding. Floors are swept and the garden weeded. While Lindsey washes the cocker spaniel I pick flowers and pop them in old sandwich spread jars and place them throughout the house. I spy Lindsey washing the car so I wash out Errol's spit bucket. Then one morning I wake up with a perfect argument. I make Mum and Dad a breakfast tray of cereal and coffee as if it's Mothers' Day and Fathers' Day combined. Walking backwards and forwards at the end of their bed I present my case.

'I have been in the family the longest, and like Karen being the longest serving girl, I am the longest serving boy and have first rights.' I can see Lindsey listening from the hallway. 'Even though Rayley is the eldest girl, Karen got her own room, so why can't I?'

Mum and Dad convene a special meeting to announce the winner. They decide because Lindsey and Errol are blood brothers, it will be better to keep them in the same bedroom so they can bond. The room is mine.

Invitation

Lindsey calls his first ever tree meeting to be held after lunch.

The backyard is in an uproar. Errol is happy because he thinks Lindsey must have remembered something important about their parents, but I suspect it has something to do with my winning the room.

At the table, Lindsey refuses to meet any of our eyes. We eat quickly and silently.

After washing up the plates, Errol makes himself a plaited head-band out of strips of curtain material, and I drape an old sheet about my shoulders as a cape in case I need something to hide under.

At three o'clock we head over to Lindsey's place. I can see him through the chinks in the boards testing his weight, pulling things down and setting things up. When he is satisfied he looks over the edge.

'Come on up.'

In an orderly fashion we climb the ladder. I'm amazed to find Lindsey has created a room in the middle of the tree with an old door and other bits of wood. He even has real furnishings.

'Please sit down.'

Karen and Beth snag the two cushions, Rayley plonks right in the middle and Errol and I sit on either side of the ladder opening. Thumbtacked to the trunk of the tree is a picture, pulled from a magazine, of a bare-chested man. He is wearing boxing gloves.

'Who's that?' Beth says.

'That's my real father, Muhammad Ali,' Lindsey says. He removes six picnic cups from their fake leather container and places them one by one along a little shelf he has made.

'He floats like a butterfly and stings like a bee,' Errol whispers. 'His hands can't hit what his eyes can't see.'

'Ladies,' Lindsey says, holding up a shiny cup and a bottle. 'Drink?'

'Yes please!'

'Today is a celebration,' Lindsey says.

'Because you found your father?' Karen says.

'No. I've known that for a while. This is about something else.'

Here it comes.

'Because of you I didn't get my own room,' Lindsey states coldly, mid-pour. I drop my head and cross my arms drawing my cape about myself.

I hear him hand the drinks out. I hear the girls say thank-you.

'David,' he asks politely. 'Red drink?'

I look up to see Lindsey standing in the green gloom.

If I say 'Yes,' he might put a dead caterpillar in my drink and grab me by the throat, the way he did to Errol, and make me swallow it. If I say 'No,' he might throw me over the edge.

'I'm sorry about the room,' I say quietly.

'No. We had a fair fight and you won.' He turns from me, puts the cup down and faces Errol. 'No, it was Errol's fault. Errol, you are

45

not my blood brother. You will never be my brother. Get out of my tree.'

Errol, still wearing his headband, falls half way down the ladder as if he's been punched. *Floats like a butterfly and stings like a bee.* He hits the ground and a sob comes out of him. He's fallen a long way. He stumbles into a run and my view of him is cut off by the serrated edges of the foliage.

*

I fashion a **Do Not Disturb** sign to hang from my bedroom door-knob. The room has a cupboard that I never have to share and a full-length mirror embedded in the door. I can stand in front of it and practice bowing and curtseying in private.

Pus

It's when Lindsey is pushing me between the house stumps with his rifle that I catch a dagger of black wood under the skin of my hand. There is no blood. The splinter acts like a plug. If it's removed the curse will be activated and I will bleed to death.

I fold my fingers over it. After a week I can only see the faintest outline of the splinter buried in all the white. I think the white means clean.

Halfway through the second week Mum notices I'm only using one hand. She tries to grab me but I am too quick. She directs Lindsey to catch me. Lindsey watches me moving. He is a lion. He tricks me into thinking he is going one way so I run the other. How could I be so stupid? He catches me and wrestles me down onto the hallway carpet.

Levering up each finger Mum reveals the white dome growing in my palm.

She gasps.

'It's white,' I yell. 'It must be clean.'

'It's pus! You could die from blood poisoning.'

'I'm going to die anyway!' I screech, turning my head to the wall.

'What are you talking about?'

'He's got a disease,' Lindsey says.

'What disease?' Mum says, shaking my shoulder. 'Come on, tell me! What disease?'

I bravely face her.

'Homo . . . ?' I'm no longer sure how to pronounce the bleeding disease.

'No!' Mum says. 'Don't say it.'

We lock eyes. She knows that I know.

'Lindsey. Hold him while I get a needle.' Mum's voice takes on a strange dead tone. 'We will get it out.'

'No, no, no, no, no, no, no!' But it's no use, Lindsey has both my wrists pinioned to the carpet.

I can hear the bathroom tap running while Mum sterilises the needle. These are the last sounds I will hear. I will die with dignity. I am a Romanov. My body goes limp. Annoyance flits across Lindsey's face because I've stopped struggling. At least he can no longer show off his strength to Mum. Mum kneels at my head and places my floppy hand it in her lap.

'That's my big boy. Now this won't hurt a bit. Lindsey, get off him!'

I imagine her lap filling up with blood and spilling over and her crying, 'Why? Why didn't I listen?'

'Out, out, out.' Mum bends over my hand and starts pressing down very hard on either side. She is sniffing and rubbing her eyes on her shoulder. 'Get out of my son.'

It is over and Mum holds the black splinter up like Excalibur.

'Ta da!'

I summon what remaining strength I have and look at my hand. I expect to see all the blood draining out of my body.

No blood. The curse is broken.

'It's gone,' I say in wonder. 'I'm cured!'

The week following, Mum says we are to spend a special day together in the city. I imagine the trip is Mum making amends for having treated me like any other kid, and not as one of the Romanovs.

Halfway into the train journey (to show I'll allow some things to stay the same) I hop up and down in excitement having recognised the rooftops of the immigration houses that Mum and her family moved into after arriving from Wales.

'Look Mum, look!' I wait patiently as she slowly swings her head to where I'm pointing. 'Your first house!'

'As big as a shoebox!' I sing-song, expecting to hear her voice accompanying mine.

Silence.

I turn in surprise.

'You didn't say it.'

'You are too close to me,' she whispers with a line of tears in her eyes, and for a split second I know she is going to abandon me.

'What do you mean?'

'The reason we're going into town is for you to see a doctor.'

This is a good idea. I can confirm with the doctor that the curse is broken. We disembark at Central and walk down the hill into the guts of the city. We catch a lift up into a skyscraper and wait in a thin brown waiting room. I've never been in a skyscraper before and I'm surprised the interior of the doctor's office is so boring. A bald man wearing glasses and a tan suit ushers us in. Through the slats of the window blind I can see other offices in other tall buildings.

'Now what can I do for you?'

Mum perches up on the very edge of her chair.

'My son is a homosexual,' she says, tears trickling down her face.

Did she say haemophilia? It sounded similar, but it also sounded like it had something to do with the sex word. I wonder if it is related to haemophilia. Maybe the curse isn't broken but has turned into something else.

'He hides picture books of movie stars under his mattress and curtseys and blows kisses to himself in the mirror. He's afraid of everything and turns hysterical at having a splinter removed.'

The doctor lowers himself down onto his haunches in front of me. His tan covered knees stretch out towards me like sphinx paws.

'I'm going to ask some questions,' he says with breath straight from a grave, 'and I don't want you to be scared. Is that okay?'

I nod.

'Do you think about boys' penises?' he asks gently.

'What?'

'Willies,' he says. 'Do you think about boys' willies?'

Nowhere have I imagined a doctor asking me this. I'm cemented in shock. His question is the type we've continually been warned about.

Remember the Beaumont children. If anybody ever asks you about your private parts or anything to do with theirs you're to run and run and run and not look back. Do you hear me?

Mum is crying as if I'm already dead.

I remember all the men's willies at the State Emergency Service barbecue, when the adults skinny-dipped after we'd gone to bed, and the giddy feeling looking at them through the upstairs louvres gave me.

'No, that's disgusting. Never.'

Scheduled Fee

'Am I covered for a D&C?' A woman's voice, devoid of emotion in my earpiece.

I ask if she has a medical item number. Every inpatient procedure has a medical item number prescribed by the government. I don't know what a D&C is. Health funds rely on medical item numbers and not names of procedures to ascertain cover. I say the word *ascertain* like I imagine a medical professional would.

'No I haven't got a number,' she says impatiently.

I tell her I can't review her coverage unless she has a medical item number. I explain that I can only give basic information at this stage, that the government and the health fund will combine to pay the scheduled fee, but no more than the scheduled fee if covered, but first we need to *ascertain* whether the procedure is covered, and for that I need a medical item number.

'I don't know what you are talking about.'

I ask whether there is someone behind a desk nearby, a nurse perhaps, who she can ask for the medical item number.

'No there isn't,' she sobs.

I tell her again that without an item number I can't tell if she has the appropriate level of cover.

'I'm standing in a phone box with a dead baby inside me,' she says, her tone rising, 'and you can't tell me if I'm covered for the removal? I shouldn't have to do this. I shouldn't have to do this.'

Saliva floods my mouth. I'm not a doctor. I'm a call centre worker. A D&C is the removal of a dead foetus. Once upon a time a woman with a dead foetus inside her didn't have to ring up health funds and talk to idiots to find out if she is covered.

MEDICAL ITEM NUMBER 35639
UTERUS, CURETTAGE OF, WITH OR WITHOUT
DILATION (INCLUDING CURETTAGE FOR
INCOMPLETE MISCARRIAGE) UNDER GENERAL
ANAESTHESIA, OR UNDER EPIDURAL OR
SPINAL (INTRATHECAL) NERVE BLOCK WHERE
UNDERTAKEN IN A HOSPITAL.
(ANAES.)
SCHEDULE FEE: $121.85

Bullet Holes

Early one morning after Dad has left for work, Mum comes in and whispers for me to meet with her in her room. I hear her going from room to room waking the others. When we enter, Mum is sitting on her bed brushing her hair.

'I'm leaving your father. I don't love him. I'm in love with Ron. The choice you have to make is if you want to come to the new house with me, or stay. You have to choose.'

My head is full of bullet holes:

- new house
- leaving your father
- in love with Ron
- stay
- you have to choose.

Mum resumes dragging her brush through her hair. It's the sound of bodies being moved.

'Before you give your answer, you each have one question.'

She lowers her brush to the bed and releases it, bristle side up.

'Starting with you because you are closest.' Mum places her hand gently along Errol's arm.

Closest? Does she mean closest as in standing to her, or closest to her heart?

'Is the dog coming?' Errol asks.

'Of course the dog is coming, silly,' Mum says, 'as if I would leave the dog!'

But you're leaving Dad.

'Should we pack all of our school things if we are going to go to a new school?' Rayley asks sensibly. 'Different schools teach things in different order.'

Rayley is calm and I realise, after having had four other families, she's the most prepared of all of us.

'I think you should bring all your school things,' Mum says.

'Will I still have my own room?' I blurt.

'You'll have to wait till you get there to find that out,' Mum says with a soft smile.

'Is the dog coming?' Beth asks innocently, giving us room to laugh.

'Oh, Beth!' Rayley says. 'Haven't you been listening?'

'Whatever happens we'll still be able to laugh,' Mum says, looking at us all like she's proud.

'Is Dad coming?' Karen asks.

We all look at Mum.

'No darling, but you'll be able to see him on weekends and school holidays.'

Lindsey doesn't have a question.

'Put up your hands those of you that are coming, and let me tell you right now I expect to count six hands.'

Slowly at first, but then spurred on by not wanting to be seen choosing Dad over Mum we all raise our hands, and then some of us, including me, raise up both.

Mum breathes a huge sigh then bursts into tears.

We are told to pack our things and to be brave. A noise outside draws us to the window. A giant orange and black wasp is manoeuvring its abdomen backwards down our drive. No one seems surprised. I look again. It's Ron reversing an orange and black painted hire trailer. Our leaving is true. We are leaving the palace.

What with all the luggage and furniture there will be too many of us to travel to the new house. It has previously been decided that Mum and the three girls will travel by train, and us boys will travel with Ron to help unload when we get there.

'You'll feel better soon,' Rayley says confidentially.

When Ron drives Mum and the girls to the train station, Lindsey purposely re-enters the house and stands waiting by the little cast-iron telephone table with the furry seat that Mum decided to leave.

'Your father will need somewhere to sit when he rings you.'

The table reminds me of a little, tethered goat villagers used to attract and kill a man-eating tiger in a movie I once saw. I can't imagine Dad sitting on it. Then I notice Lindsey's finger resting against the plastic arrow on the address book. Lindsey's finger slowly and deliberately moves the arrow down to W.

Dad's work.

'Stop. You'll get into trouble.'

As these words leave my mouth I can't tell where this trouble will come from. Nearly everyone, bar Dad, is doing something they shouldn't.

The three of us disengage from the telephone table and float through the house. Bits from the exploded laundry cupboard are strewn across the floor. The kitchen floor is a mess of abandoned Tupperware and buckled cooking trays. All the big pieces of furniture are gone. It's as if the house has lost its mind. We open the back door and look out over the backyard. All our trees look the same. I wish I could fold up the view like a picnic blanket. We descend the stairs to say goodbye.

'I'm leaving you, my beautiful tree,' I whisper, with my head against the trunk. 'Thank you for being my friend. I will never forget you.'

I don't want to leave Dad, or my tree, or my room. Part of me wants to run and hide and only come out when the others have gone, but the thought of crawling out into a house without Mum being there is a thought too terrible to contemplate. It's Dad I have to lose.

I am going.

Ron's car and hire trailer slide to a stop out the front and he beeps the horn. The three of us race back upstairs.

'I love you, I love you, I love you,' I call in a panic, running from room to room.

In the car I sit closest to Ron. Almost touching. Lindsey and Errol have the dog straddling their laps.

I catch Ron's penetrating black eyes in the rear vision mirror and he tells me to get him a cigarette from the glove box. I lean across Errol and Lindsey's legs, press open the little door and remove his cigarettes. Ron's meaty hands remain clamped to the wheel and he motions with his head for me to put one in his mouth. His eyes compel me. I lift the cardboard lid and lever one out by its caramel tip and insert it between his lips. My hand is shaking. Ron snorts and pushes the lighter button in with a fat, dirty finger.

He is Rasputin.

Oprah

'Welcome to Physician Health. My name is David. How can I help you?'

'I'd like to know how much dental benefit my kids have got left.'

'Can I have your membership number?'

'Get down! No, outside. Sorry about this but my dog is in the house. I have to put the phone down.'

'Of course,' I laugh, 'it sounds like you've got a handful there.'

'You can say that again!' she says in pretend exasperation.

The woman sounds nice and relaxed, like someone I could be friends with.

The receiver clatters to the counter top and I hear the woman try to round up her dog. These are the type of calls I like, the ones that act as a window into other people's everyday lives. I hear a screen door open.

'Oprah, outside!'

I hear the door slam and footsteps as she moves back towards the phone.

'You know why we call her Oprah?' she says, like she's known me forever. 'She's a black bitch!'

Wellington Point

Our new house is on a hill with a yard full of fruit trees. Except for a frangipani, they are not large enough to climb. The house had once been divided into flats and the three girls are to sleep in one of the old kitchens. Their three beds are placed over the footprints of the oven, the fridge and the sink. Lindsey and Errol share the middle room that can only be reached through the lounge room and I'm allocated the little front room with louvered windows that catch the breeze from the sea.

Ron fixes his C.B. radio equipment above a recliner chair placed dead centre in the house, and erects aerials on the roof so he can monitor all the emergency channels. From his seated position nothing goes on, inside or out, that Ron isn't aware of. Walking home from school, the house with its waving antennas looks like the carapace of some gigantic awful insect, and it feels strange knowing Mum is going to bed with a man who isn't Dad.

Chased

Ron never gives warning. One moment he's leaning back in his recliner chair sipping instant coffee and smoking a cigarette and next he's lunging out with the lightning reflexes of a trap-door spider. The time he lunges for me I manage to duck under his arm and hightail it through the back door and down the covered back stairs. I hear the others scatter as he launches himself in enraged pursuit. He sounds like a freight train. I flee up the side of the house to the roadway. The tips of his fingers rake the air behind my neck. There is no one on the street to intervene. His breathing begins to labour. He isn't built for a sustained chase. He's too old and a smoker. I pray for a heart attack so he'll drop down dead.

He slams into overdrive.

My only chance is an abandoned block where an old house has been bulldozed. I zigzag through the rubble and debris. I skip and jump. Ron can't keep up. Physical distance cracks open. I see the jagged peaks of a broken bottle a split second before my right foot lands.

I collapse into a hollow of broken bricks and clutch the wound. It's bad. Blood seeps through my fingers. Ron laughs a sinister laugh and steps up onto the edge of the hollow. I let go my foot and cover my face with bloody hands. Nothing happens. Why hasn't he started? I crack open red fingers. He is looking down with a weird look of confusion and pain as if he's standing on a castle's parapet and taken an arrow in the back.

He stumbles away and I hobble home bleeding. I get six stitches at the local medical centre. No punishment for that perceived infringement ever eventuates.

Something happened in that abandoned lot and I don't know what, or why.

*

A few weeks later Mum meets us at the front door with a grim set to her lips and announces she wants to speak to us in her bedroom. Shucking off my school bag I'm happy; meeting in the bedroom must mean she has changed her mind about Ron and we're going home. From all the shy smiles us kids secretly exchange I can tell we're all thinking the same thing.

Mum is sitting on the bed waiting for us all to enter and then she jumps up laughing and clapping her hands. 'Just joking! I'm not sad! I'm the happiest I've been in my whole life. I'm pregnant with twins. It's a miracle.'

Rasputin could perform miracles and here he's done it again. He's made my mother pregnant. My father couldn't do it, and that's why we were all adopted and fostered. There is a look on my mother's face I've never seen before. It's like she is seeing the full extent of the Romanov treasure chest for the first time.

In the vault of my mother's heart we're all tipped out onto black velvet to be re-graded. She raises up a jeweller's monocled eye. I am terrified she'll discover I'm nothing but a cubic zirconia because the true diamonds are in her belly.

*

To prepare for the expansion Ron trades his car in for a small bus that once belonged to a local orphanage, and on weekends Mum arranges bonding excursions between Ron and us. We're the only kids who need a bus to be driven round in. We slouch down and hide our faces behind hands or books until we are suburbs away from being seen by anyone from our new schools.

The first trip is to Bullen's African Lion Park. We spend more time in the children's playground than on safari trying to differentiate a scrawny lion from a discarded, hessian sack. The only interesting thing is the liger, even though it's sterile like Dad.

Our usual destination is a finger of land called Wellington Point that spears out into Moreton Bay. When the tide is low a red sand pathway a kilometre long opens up to a small island called King Island.

'The first one to the island will be King,' Mum says, readying a tea towel for a starter's flag.

At first I imagined my Romanov ghosts would respond like bulls to red flags to this challenge and buoy me across the red sand pathway on invisible arms, but each time I'm left floundering in the wake of Lindsey and Errol.

On our fourth visit, Ron, who has been sitting watching the competition, seizes Lindsey and Errol by their arms and holds them back.

'GO!' he yells to me like we're teammates in a running relay.

I don't want the Romanovs to use Ron, but I know this is my only chance.

I make it halfway across the sand bridge before Ron lets Lindsey and Errol go, but neither attempts to catch me. When I make it to the top of the island's first small dune I perform a half-hearted Indian dance.

On the way home Mum tells Ron he shouldn't have held the boys back. That I have to win on my own merits, or not at all. Even though it's about me, it feels good to hear Ron getting into trouble. He keeps telling her to stop telling him what to do, but Mum keeps on at him like she used to do at Dad. Ron veers the bus off the road towards a eucalyptus tree. He skids the bus to a halt at the very last second. As the dust settles, and in the stillness of the gently rocking vehicle, everyone can see Ron has lined the tree up exactly with Mum's pregnant belly.

Then Ron's wife says Ron can look after their three sons for a while.

2nd diagram of the sleeping arrangements once Ron's three boys
and the twins arrive:

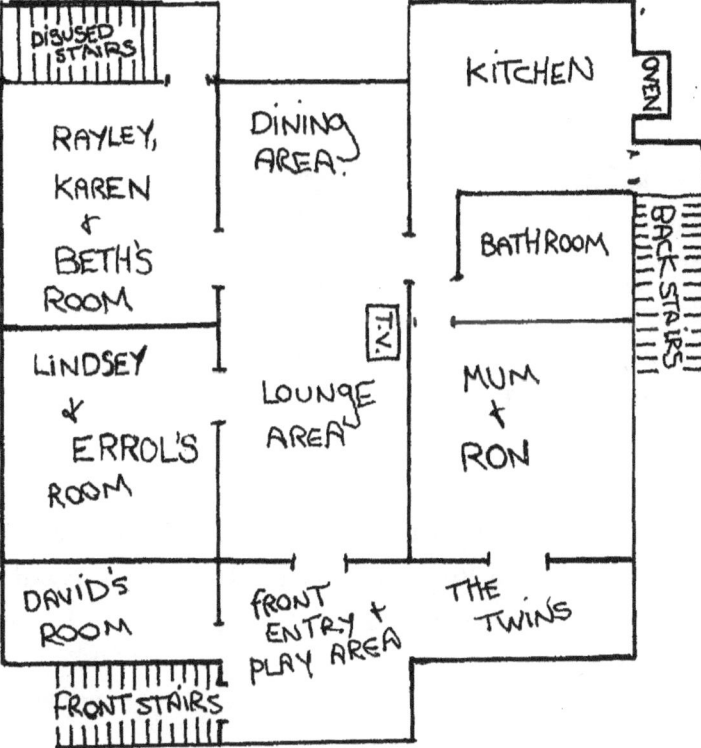

DISUSED STAIRS

RAYLEY,
KAREN
&
BETH'S
ROOM

DINING
AREA

KITCHEN

OVEN

BATHROOM

BACK STAIRS

LINDSEY
&
ERROL'S
ROOM

T.V.

LOUNGE
AREA

MUM
&
RON

DAVID'S
ROOM

FRONT
ENTRY &
PLAY AREA

THE
TWINS

FRONT STAIRS

DOWNSTAIRS ROOM
DIRECTLY BELOW
LOUNGE & FRONT
ENTRY WHERE
RON'S BOYS SLEEP

SHOWER

LOO

SINK

By age the kids descend like this:

- Stepbrother 1
- Lindsey
- Errol
- Stepbrother 2
- David (me)
- Stepbrother 3
- Rayley
- Karen
- Beth
- Newborn twin 1
- Newborn twin 2.

But keeping a list of who's who is now pointless. There is no sibling hierarchy; there is only Ron, who has started to use his fists and feet to keep us boys in line. For the girls, I find out later, he uses something else.

Sasha

I always assumed I would be the first to be sought out by a blood relative, but when the authorities contact Mum, it's to arrange a meeting between Lindsey, Errol, and their blood sister Sasha. Sasha has been refusing to eat until she sees her brothers again, and her foster parents are at their wits end.

On the chosen Saturday we mill about the yard so as not to miss her arrival. Lindsey is down along the back fence pulling out a small, dead tree, and Errol is sitting at the bottom of the steps playing with the dog. Karen and Beth are stretched out in the branches of the frangipani, and Rayley is sitting on the fence closest to the gate. So I can look busy I position myself in the stand of banana trees with the machete and rake.

A car turns into our corner and slides to a halt. Lindsey and Errol disappear under the house, and Ron's sons wander out like unconvincing decoys.

Three people, two big and one small, stay sitting in the car looking at us through their rolled-up windows. The woman in the front is trying to make it look like she isn't saying the things that she is to the small one in the back. The girl has a determined set to her head: she stopped listening to the woman a long time ago. I won't be surprised if they drive off, but the back door swings open and two sandals pop out.

Sasha, because it must be Sasha, stands on the grassy verge looking down and straightening her dress. A purple satin headband dotted with diamonds restrains her hair and catches sunlight. Her lilac dress has white flowers on it. Everything is matching. Karen, Beth and Rayley look agog. These people must be rich. Only princesses in fairy stories wear all matching. Sasha lifts her head like she's finished saying a prayer before dinner. Her eyes sample each of us in turn. She looks calm and very pretty, but I notice her fingers are clamped to the edges of her dress.

She finds me standing stock-still among the banana trees but her eyes don't stay long. Her eyes start to skip back over our faces to check she hasn't missed anyone. I wonder if she is holding up a mental picture of Errol's face against each of ours like a snapshot.

None of us call out to tell her that her brothers are hiding under the house. Her eyes drop. Her fingers start to worry at the side seams of her skirt.

I picture a perfect diamond hidden in the hem.

'Sasha!' Mum calls. 'Welcome.'

At the sight of an adult the two people in the car crank open their doors and step out. Mum registers the look on Sasha's face and grabs her in a fierce hug and calls out, 'Where are those two fool boys? Lindsey, Errol, your sister's here!'

Sasha shoots Mum a hungry smile.

The boys edge out from under the house, but neither moves towards their sister.

'Come here,' Mum says, making gathering motions. 'She won't

bite! Will you Sasha?'

The girl shakes her head and tries to cover her smile but it spreads out on either side of her thumb and little finger.

Mum takes hold of the boys' shoulders and draws the three of them together. Lindsey and Errol drop their heads as if they're wilting. Mum steps back surveying her handiwork and walks towards the gate where Sasha's foster parents are waiting.

Lindsey and Errol stay cast in the shape Mum has put them into for only as long as it takes for the adults to disappear upstairs, and then they crack apart leaving Sasha standing alone.

It is obvious the boys don't know the protocol of long-lost reunions. It's a complete waste. Neither knows to grab Sasha in a joyous hug and swing her round and round, laughing heartily at the sky. Neither knows to take her by the arm, one each, and squire her about the yard pointing out non-consequential things, while trying to ignore the special feeling of touch. Neither knows to swear undying devotion and promise never to be apart again.

I know from the look on her face that Sasha plays the same sorts of games I play. I want to ask her what she remembers about her real mother and father. I bet I wouldn't be disappointed. I bet all her stories have beginnings, middles and ends.

Laughter floats down from upstairs as the adults compare notes on what it's like raising kids not your own. Mum comes down with sandwiches and drinks for us all, but Sasha picks up a sandwich like it's a folded leaf and only pretends to eat. Lindsey and Errol remain shadowy figures under the house.

'Sasha,' I offer from the banana glade, 'do you want to come and play?'

She shakes her head.

The afternoon drags on.

The three of us grow tired waiting in the banana grove. But at least we are in the shade. Sasha is sitting in full sun twiddling a stick.

'She must be getting awfully hot,' Beth says, her chin resting in her hand.

'She must be getting awfully bored,' I say.

'But what can we do?' Karen says.

'Let's put on a show for her,' Rayley says, in a marvelling tone. 'Let's play Brown Snake!'

'Good idea Rayley,' I say, 'but I don't know how to play Brown Snake. Let's do the Romanovs. Let's start under the frangipani tree where we can all pretend to be sewing jewels in our clothes.'

'Who'll play the soldiers?' Karen whispers. 'You know none of the boys will – they think our games are for babies.'

'We can die here in the grove,' I say, looking round, 'and pretend the banana trees are the soldiers.'

We break cover and run to the frangipani tree.

'Ladies and . . . ' I gasp, in pretend shock, ' . . . and no gentlemen. But that doesn't matter because you dear lady are about to witness the greatest story ever told.'

Sasha shows no interest.

'Introducing Rayley as Grand Princess Olga.'

Rayley curtsies.

I pretend to be on the verge of clapping but change my mind.

'Please,' I dampen down the empty air with my hands, 'save your applause. In . . . tro . . . ducing Karen as Grand Princess Tatiana, and Beth as Grand Princess Anastasia.'

The four of us clap and cheer.

'Alas, there are four sisters in this drama but we are missing a person to play Grand Princess Maria – is there a lovely lady in the audience who would be so kind as to join us?'

Sasha keeps her eyes focused on the ground.

'No? Oh well.'

'And last but not least I shall be playing the dual role of soldier, and Crown Prince Alexei. Oh yeah, and introducing the banana trees who will play the soldiers whose only desire is to kill us.'

Sasha looks up.

'Let the show begin!' I say.

We huddle beneath the frangipani tree sewing jewels into our clothes. Anastasia pricks her finger and sobs.

Grand Duchess Tatiana leaps to her feet and rages at the brutality of the soldiers.

Olga starts to talk but I interrupt her.

'Oh, woe is us!' I say. 'We are being held prisoner in this strange house and I'm scared we'll be killed by the soldiers of the revolution.' Behind me the three grand Duchesses break out sobbing.

Grabbing the rake I transform into a soldier.

'Now I'm a soldier.'

Yelling rude words I usher the girls across the yard and into the banana trees.

'Please don't kill us, please don't kill us.' Rayley is on her hands and knees, beseeching the banana trees.

'It's no use.' I turn to my sisters for one last look. 'Goodbye cruel world!'

'NhNhNhNhNhNhNhNhNhNhNhNhNhNh!' Saliva bullets

spray everywhere from the backs of our throats. We writhe about tossing our bodies against the trunks. Then the gunfire stops and we start moaning and screaming.

For the first time in history the story takes a different turn.

'Fight back!' Beth cries, in a voice not her own, and we galvanise.

It's as if the rubies, emeralds, and diamonds we've sewn into our clothes crystallise into impenetrable shells that cover our bodies.

We are super-human. Our hair transforms into shiny helmets and our eyes and teeth glitter. Taking hold of the machete and other tools left lying among the dead leaves we rise up. We attack the trees, slicing through their uniforms and into crisp flesh. Watery sap runs down the trunks and banana leaves fall like real human arms. We are screaming with rage at the soldiers for the years of getting away with killing us. We are hysterical. Sasha is laughing and clapping her hands.

All the boys reappear from under the house. Lindsey and Errol laugh alongside Sasha. Our screaming draws the adults out onto the back landing, but instead of everyone melting into one big, happy party, Sasha's foster parents hurry downstairs and without a word seize Sasha and lead her through the side gate to the car.

This was the first and last time I ever saw Sasha, the girl who was supposed to be our sister.

After they've gone, Mum yells I've embarrassed the whole family and that I'm too old to be playing stupid games.

'For God's sake, grow up!'

All right, I'll grow up.

I wait until she goes shopping. I enter her and Ron's room and rifle through her papers in her bedside drawer looking for the information about my real family. I find a small diary buried at the bottom.

There on the very last page are two sentences.

'The nurse said David's birth mother was 13 when she gave birth,' says the first sentence.

'David's hospital bracelet has him named as Mark Fisher,' says the second.

Mark Fisher.

My real name is Mark Fisher, and my birth mother was 13 years old.

Little Confidant

The first child to get a bullet is Rayley. A phone call is made and a car from the orphanage is sent to collect her. I'm home from school pretending to be sick because Mum informed me of what is about to happen. I'm still Mum's little confidant.

Mum stands at the top of the stairs staring down while Rayley struggles to pull herself away from the grip of the man and the woman who've taken hold of her. Mum's excuse why we couldn't have Rayley anymore is that she'd caught her stealing from her purse.

The car drove away with Rayley's small, pale face looking out.

*

As Lindsey and Errol grow taller and stronger, Ron evolves from using his fists and feet to using a plank of wood. He also designates a special area to enact his disciplinary measures. Because of the low lintel Ron can't use the garage for parking the bus so he turns the space into his boxing ring. He flings one or both boys over the ancient oil mark in the centre of the cement floor and then closes the garage doors behind him. After the bolt is driven home, the rest of us listen from the stand of recuperating banana trees to the dull thuds, grunts, and the boy's screamed apologies cut short. Our eyes and ears are drawn from the garage to the kitchen doorway where Mum is standing. She never comes down. She never tries to stop him.

Lindsey is not the same after these sessions in the garage. It's as if Ron has beaten more than just his flesh. It's as if he's knocked the image of his chosen father, Muhammad Ali, right out of him.

Ron never uses the wood on me, just his fists and feet, and I never see the insides of the garage the way Lindsey and Errol do. I do see the deep purple bruises on their skin, and I do see them try to walk tall and straight without surrendering to their injuries. I also notice Ron's sons move about bruise free.

Driven to pull the trigger on themselves, Lindsey and Errol are the second and third to receive their bullets. Before they leave, Errol comes into my room and asks if I want to run away too.

'No,' I say, 'I'll tough it out.'

Lindsey and Errol walk stiffly away from home on the same night, but on opposite sides of the road.

While everyone else in the house sleeps, I watch through the cracked-open louvres of my bedroom as my brothers slip away.

Leotard

Years later, after the full extent of his violence was known, I asked my mother why Ron did what he did.

'It's the cycle of abuse,' she said.

My mother had recently started a degree in Social Work via correspondence and was up with all the current theories.

'It's self-perpetuating,' she said. 'When Ron was a little boy, back in England, his mother enrolled him in ballet classes. One day, he was walking home in his little flesh coloured leotard, and some teenage boys coaxed him into an overgrown bomb site, a leftover from the Blitz. He was gang-raped.'

'But why grow up and repeat the worst thing that ever happened to you?'

'It's a phenomenon,' she says, shrugging. 'I'm not far along enough in the course to know why.'

I remember the day he chased me into the overgrown block. How he'd looked like he'd seen a ghost. Was it the ghost of himself as a little boy lying defiled in the broken bricks of a bomb site?

Maybe I should feel sorry for him, but I don't. The fact that he was haunted saved me that day from a flogging, or worse. But it never protected the others.

State of Origin

In the last half hour of my shift a woman rings the health fund and asks if she's covered for psychiatric care.

'I need to commit myself,' she says.

'Before we go any further I need your details. What is your name and membership number?'

'Josephine Allard. 4593268.'

One look at the policy onscreen and I inwardly groan. Josephine isn't covered for psychiatric care. I tell her psychiatric conditions are one of her restrictions and she has to rely on the public hospital system. Between sobs and gasps for air Josephine tells me her doctor told her that the public system doesn't have any room in its wards. She tells me she has just confronted the man who abused her throughout her childhood and now she wants to kill herself. My voice chases after hers, repeating she doesn't have health cover for private inpatient psychiatric care and if she increases her cover then she'll have to wait two months for pre-existing conditions. She is crying a hopeless sound. There is nothing I can do. I fall silent. I slide my eyes from her details to the laminated card stuck to the side of the monitor, 'Life is not measured by the number of breaths we take, but by the moments that take our breath away.' I wonder if this moment qualifies.

I want to take the card and rip it into a million pieces, but I can't because it's not mine. The desk's official inhabitant will note the loss and I'll be asked in an accusatory tone if I took it. I would like to punch the person in the throat who dreamt up this smug saying. I lower my voice to a half-whisper so my co-workers can't hear and I congratulate Josephine on her bravery. I tell her about Ron and how scared I was of him and how I never had the guts to confront him. That if she goes ahead and hurts herself it proves he still has power over her. That she needs to stand up and fight, that she already has taken the hardest step by confronting him.

Josephine sniffles, says goodbye and lowers the phone. I wonder if she's going off to 'do the deed' and whether I should call the police, but I'm sure that would be breaching privacy laws.

Following particularly disturbing calls we are allowed by management to take a maximum of 10 minutes off the phones to calm down. There's even a room with a bed, but it's better to climb the stairs to the call-centre roof, to gaze at the lit cathedral and breathe the night air.

After my shift I arrive home to a dark and empty house. Jason is still at work at the old people's home. I move from room to room. The surface of my skin starts to itch and my breath catches. I haven't had a panic attack for years. I remember the breathing exercises my psychologist taught me to keep the attacks at bay. I remember going to her because I was scared I was going to hurt myself. She said I must be strong to have survived the violence of my childhood. I remember laughing and saying my strength was in my ability to divorce myself from reality. How creating worlds where I am more than I really am kept me sane. How, as a child, I'd fantasised about being a Romanov. Telling her this, I thought I was being charming.

From the opposite side of the desk she wrote on her pad, *delusions of grandeur?*

I turn on the television to try and take my mind off Josephine Allard, and the psychologist who thought I was delusional. Mindless football. The State of Origin competition between the State of Queensland where all the bad things happened to my family and the State of New South Wales where I now live. The first game. Focusing on the television I lose track of my place in the breathing exercise. They never worked much for me anyway. What works is standing in front of the panic attack and screaming COME ON, and punching the air like Lleyton Hewitt. Dare it to come and it usually backs down.

GO THE BLUES! I want the blue-wearing New South Welshmen to slaughter the maroon-wearing team from Queensland. I am a traitor to my home state.

The camera pans over a huddle of Maroon players and catches the quadruple capital Xs – the cartoon sign for poison and the trademark of the famous Queensland beer worn across the bicep of each Queensland player.

I should have stabbed Ron. I should have killed him when I had the chance, but unlike Josephine Allard I'm a coward. I could never have confronted him.

The walls of the Queensland stadium are covered in human supporters all wearing maroon clothes. A commentator refers to the stadium as 'The Cauldron', and with all the flashbulbs going off it does look like the insides of a barbecue. From the throats of thousands of Maroon supporters comes the three-part scream, *Queens-lan-der*, *Queens-lan-der*. The sound roils from one wall of the stadium to the other and back again like a gigantic wave. A few pockets of Blues supporters can be spotted struggling in the maroon flood, waving plastic blow-up blue hands as if they're drowning. My hair stands on end.

At half time it's 18-6 and the Blues are winning. They're setting themselves up to romp home and I settle back into the cushions to watch Queensland get crushed. During the break one of the commentators warns there's a history of Queensland comebacks. I know nothing about Queensland football's glorious past, but I have to scoff. Even I know Queensland can't come back from 18-6.

In the 50th minute Inglis scores for Queensland and Thurston converts taking the score to 18-12. Both are Aboriginal players and I wonder whether they are torn playing for the State where so many bad things happened to their race. They're ecstatic. In the 58th minute Queensland and New South Wales are tied. The commentators are raving about the Queensland spirit and one of them is screaming hysterically.

'If you invite a Queenslander in he never leaves!'

At the 60-minute mark a New South Wales player throws a wobbly pass straight into the arms of an opposition player who immediately scores. The score is Queensland 22 to New South Wales 18. The crowd is roaring. The commentator is having some sort of epileptic fit.

'You invite a Queenslander in, he'll set up camp, he'll eat you out of house and home, he'll drink your beer and eat everything in your cupboards. He'll never go!'

With 11 minutes left Thurston kicks a field goal taking the score to 25-18. The number of patrons in the cauldron has been calculated and flashes across the screen: 52,498. There is nothing New South Wales can do.

My adopted state has lost. The roar of QUEENS-LAN-DER sounds throughout the house.

There are three games in the series and New South Wales can still come back and win it. I count on it, and curse Queensland.

*

An embossed card arrives in the mail inviting *Jason and Partner* to a wedding in Noosa, Queensland. The bride-to-be is a distant relative of Jason's. On the map Cherbourg looks to be about two and a half hours away from Noosa in a north-westerly direction. This is my chance. Errol may only have left Cherbourg temporarily. Once I've attended the wedding I can head inland and try to find him.

I could ring the police station again and ask if Errol is a permanent Cherbourg resident but I don't think Errol would appreciate me ringing the cops. The trial of Sergeant Chris Hurley over the death of Mulrunji Doomadgee is in full swing. After an altercation with Sergeant Hurley on Palm Island turned violent, Doomadgee was discovered dead in a holding cell.

I ring Beth at the Brisbane pub where she is the gaming manager in charge of all the poker machines and ask if she wants to come to Noosa for a few days and help me find Errol. My sister and Jason get on. Both smoke dope and love reality television programs. Dope makes me think people are out to kill me and I have to hurt them first, and, unless the participants are naked, reality TV bores me.

I tell Beth I'd like her to drive me to Cherbourg.

Beth is dating a guy called Jeff who works in the same pub. I hear her tell him over the ding, ding, ding of the poker machines that I want her to drive me to Cherbourg. Jeff is Aboriginal and I hear him laugh and warn her off. He says he's been to Cherbourg and knows what he's talking about.

'Tell Jeff,' I yell into the handpiece, 'that there's an emu farm in Cherbourg that's a tourist attraction. We could just go there and ask questions!'

Beth relays this to Jeff and he yells so I can hear him. 'The emu farm isn't open anymore. It got closed down.'

Damn.

I'd had it all worked out in my head: 'Isn't the carving on this egg beautiful and intricate! Oh, by the way, do you know a guy called Errol? He's my brother I haven't seen in 20 years.'

Beth takes back the call. 'Jeff doesn't think it's a good idea to just rock up in Cherbourg asking questions.'

'They'll rush the car!' Jeff's laughing voice interrupts from the background. 'A reconnaissance team will be sent in and they'll find one of your car doors on a different car and one of your wheels on another, and they'll see people wearing your clothes but you'll never be seen again.'

I decide to limit my research to Brisbane. Maybe Errol is still in the city.

*

Friends of the bride have donated a house on one of Noosa's man-made canals for us to stay in, a house whose owner is only in Australia a couple of times a year. Directly across the water is a high-arched walk-bridge Dean Martin types could scale singing 'That's Amore'.

Because canal developments are brand new land where nothing bad has ever happened beyond the destruction of fish spawning grounds, I wonder if people living here are absolved from worrying about Australia's original inhabitants. Then I think of all the run-off from the surrounding mountains and the bodies of all the original inhabitants who would have disintegrated into the water and washed down to the river mouth where the canal development has been built and I realise nothing's new. It's all ancient.

The wedding is in the hilltop grounds of a beautiful sprawling ranch house that overlooks wetlands. The owner, a friend of the bride and groom, is a music industry bigwig and an avid art collector. A painting of a life-sized rodeo rider on a thrashing horse dominates one wall of a breezeway. Another huge piece in the living room is of an ocean wave crashing over a ship's deck.

The wedding is one of those open-seating affairs where you sit where you want to eat your meal. We find table space where the occupants are regaling each other with tales of how they'd each met their significant other. Jason starts our story by recounting how he met me when he went to Brisbane on a holiday and friends took him to a gay bar. Then he hands the reins to me.

'I'd moved back to Brisbane from Sydney to look after my mother who had cancer. I was on a Carer's Pension and living in a caravan in her backyard,' I say. 'I thought my life was over. I was a pensioner in a caravan for Christ's sake. Who'd want to go out with that?'

There are shaking heads all round.

'Anyway, I'd gone out that night with a mate who'd also relocated to Brisbane and we both saw Jason at the same time but I made the first move.'

Next it's Jason's turn.

'After about an hour David's mate came up and said, 'So, you've met David. He's had more men from this place than you've had hot dinners,'' Jason says, raising his eyebrows, and everybody at the table laughs.

'Which was a complete lie!' I say, with pretend outrage. 'Brian was just jealous!'

'Anyway,' Jason says. 'I invited David home and when we got in the taxi the driver turned around and said 'Hi David!', and then when we got back to the place I was staying I ordered pizza. When the pizza arrived the delivery guy looked over my shoulder and said, 'Hi David!', so it really did look like what his mate had said was true.'

'The taxi driver was Brian's older brother, and I went to high school with the pizza guy!' I say.

'Anyway,' Jason says. 'We've been together ever since!'

Hands down, our origin story beats all the others' but I'm conscious that we've turned ourselves into a Benny Hill joke. I wonder why we do that.

After dinner, someone passes a joint round and because I don't want to get paranoid from passive smoking I tell Jason I'm going to stretch my legs.

I walk round the side of one of the main buildings and come face to face with a traditional Aboriginal man in a loincloth aiming his spear at an abandoned shopping trolley. It's a wall stencil. The owner must have commissioned it.

A shopping trolley would never have fooled Errol. It's another cheap joke.

I walk to the edge of the lawn and look out over the wetlands to the mountains. I'm facing northwest towards Cherbourg. I'm a coward for not going all the way.

Solidarity

The reason I left Queensland and moved to New South Wales was the introduction of the 1985 Queensland Liquor Act. This law made it illegal to serve alcohol to sexual deviants (homosexuals) and was the final straw, so to speak.

Before I came back to tend to my mother's illness, the only substantial time I'd spent in Queensland was when I'd returned to see Ron sentenced for child molestation. He'd finally been caught. My only dilemma seemed to be finding a pub where I could celebrate with my deviant friends. It was on this visit that I last saw Errol.

I was sauntering through King George Square, all eyeliner and bleached hair. It was 1987. It had taken two years for Ron's case to reach the courts, and I thought he'd be going away for a long, long time.

As I walked through the square, all the oncoming pedestrians started to veer away from me. I thought it was because they couldn't abide sharing the pathway with such a proud fag.

God, I remember thinking. *Nothing ever changes in Queensland – they're still terrified of poofters.*

As if performing a magician's trick I turned dramatically to yell 'POOF!' at their scurrying backsides and came face to face with the real reason for the evacuation. Coming up from behind, casting all before them like a grader shovel, was a moving wall of 10 Aboriginal men.

I decided on the spot I wasn't going to respond like the other pedestrians. I would stand my ground. Maybe even teach the scaredy-cats a lesson. Maybe die trying. Some of the evacuees stopped in premonition of watching the silly poof be beaten to death.

'Hello David,' the biggest Aboriginal man said, smiling.

Not too shy and not a grin. Errol. My brother.

He didn't look embarrassed at what I was wearing, and none of his mates did either. Solidarity. We walked to the centre of King George Square, and while Errol and I stood talking, his gang encircled us. Pedestrians almost broke their own necks doing double takes at the biggest queen in the square talking to the biggest Aboriginal man they'd ever seen. *Gawk. Go on, gawk you racist homophobes.*

Errol said he was just out of prison and on his way to Musgrave Park. I asked what he'd done, and Errol said there'd been a fight where a man died, but he didn't elaborate. I asked him if he ever saw Lindsey, or knew what happened to him.

'Years ago, after I'd run away, I was cornered by a gang of skinheads in a back alley,' Errol said. 'And Lindsey came out of nowhere, knocked them down and disappeared before I could thank him. That was the only time.'

I told Errol about Ron and what he'd done.

Errol swallowed and looked momentarily away.

I assured him Ron would be put away for sure.

'I'm going to get him for all of us that bastard ever hurt,' he said. 'I've got a lot of brothers inside who'll do it.'

I imagined Ron being kicked and hit in the same way he used to beat Lindsey and Errol. I imagined men visiting his cell in the way he used to visit the girls' beds. I imagined Ron as frightened as he used to make me.

Errol made me memorise the phone number of the hostel where he was staying and told me to contact him as soon as I heard of Ron's sentence.

Errol's phone number was my mantra.

Ron missed out on jail time because of all his good work with the emergency services, tying down roofs after high winds and pulling animals out of storm water drains. Errol's phone number evaporated. I returned to New South Wales with my tail between my legs.

The only other time I heard anything of Errol was years later when I was working in a bar on Sydney's Oxford Street (where I drank and drank and drank). Corey, an Aboriginal guy who used to play school football with Errol, walked in. Corey told me he used to hang out with Errol in Musgrave Park and how they both ended up living in the same Aboriginal hostel. Corey told me Errol found his real family but the car that was headed to Cherbourg for the reunion was in an accident and three of Errol's brothers were killed. Corey said the rest of the reunion was cancelled and Errol had crawled under his hostel bed and didn't come out for days.

Corey is part of the AIDS quilt now, panel number 103007.

*

I need to keep track of Errol's dead:

- Mitchell Pringle (The young man who hung himself in the cell)
- Brother 1
- Brother 2
- Brother 3
- Corey.

Rhino

After the wedding Beth speeds and tailgates down the Bruce Highway waving her fist at anybody who gets in the way of delivering Jason to the airport on time. She's on a mission. In or out of the car Beth isn't scared of anything or anyone anymore. Beth is yelling over the noise of the radio about how Mum continued to harbour feelings for Ron right up until the day she died.

'Remember Mum saying how when we were kids she'd be like a lioness if anybody hurt us?' Beth asks, looking back through the rear vision mirror.

'Yeah,' I say.

'Funny how she ended up like a rhinoceros with its horn cut off standing behind a tree,' Beth says, and returns her gaze to the road.

'Those poor foster kids got it the worst,' I say. 'Especially Rayley. I was there the day she was sent away.'

'Rayley was the lucky one,' Beth says. 'You have this fantasy that being adopted is better than being fostered. Even though she's dead now, being fostered saved Rayley. It got her away from Ron. Mum couldn't give us adopted kids back. We were stuck in his constant arms' reach.'

'I've had a lot of fantasies,' I admit, remembering Anastasia.

'Do you think Mum's intention was to save Rayley by sending her away?' I say. 'Or was she protecting her own relationship with Ron?'

'Probably a bit of both,' Beth says.

We fall silent until we get to the airport.

'Good luck finding your brother,' Jason says gently. 'I wish I could stay.'

'No way!' I say. 'You've heard enough about our freaky family!'

I'm secretly glad Jason is leaving. If I find Errol I don't want to scare him with my same-sex partner.

I tell him I'll be home in one week. We hug and he disappears into the terminal.

'Do you have a street directory?' I say, returning to the car.

'Yeah, there's an ancient one under your seat,' Beth says.

While Beth negotiates our way out of the airport I flick through the maps and locate, 10 minutes away from our current position, the little black square marked ORPHANAGE.

'I want to see the children's home where we got Errol. Do you mind a detour?'

One block away from our destination the car passes a cemetery and I remember how sick Errol was when we got him.

'I wonder how many orphanage kids buried there died of grief?'

'Kids are resilient things,' Beth says.

'The ones that survive.'

'God,' Beth says, 'this is like an episode of *The X-Files*.'

'Keep going straight.'

The car comes to a T-junction and the orphanage buildings are directly across the road. The tree with the native beehive is gone.

Beth parks the car on the gravel verge and switches off the engine. Silence. There is no one about. A sign at the front gate announces the buildings are an aged care facility. Across the road from the buildings that used to be the orphanage is a huge empty block of land lined with the old fence posts and gates. The houses that once stood there look to have been obliterated.

'Speaking of the *X-Files*,' I say, pointing, 'nice old-fashioned fences, gates and driveways, but no nice old-fashioned houses.'

'NhNhNhNhNhNhNhNhNhNhNhNhNhNh,' Beth sprays the decimated area with an invisible machine gun and pretends to blow smoke out of the barrel. 'Imagine all the orphanage kids looking across at real happy families all day! Their stares would've been like flame throwers.'

'Hmmm, you wish kids had such power.'

'You betcha,' Beth says.

I feel strange looking down the sweeping driveway we drove into over 30 years ago. It feels as if I'm trespassing on Errol's story. This is all before my time.

'Let's go,' I say, getting back into the car, 'we don't belong here.'

I'm staying with Beth on the south side within walking distance of the river. Her one-bedroom fibro flat is one of five held up on a forest of stumps and looks to be about 100 years old. Beth gives me her room and says she'll be happy on the couch. She won't take no for an answer.

I decide to visit Musgrave Park on the off-chance Errol might be there. I don't know if I'm being insulting thinking Errol might still be hanging round the park but I can't risk leaving this avenue unexplored. Beth drops me at the station and I scan the ticket machine for Vulture Street train station. The station isn't listed. I approach the stationmaster's window and I'm told through the gap that the city fathers changed the name to South Bank when Brisbane hosted EXPO. Vulture Street sounded too ugly.

'That's a shame,' I say, handing through money for the ticket. 'When I was a kid Vulture Street always made me look twice for birds of prey waiting to swoop.'

'Every kid did,' the stationmaster says.

Two stations later I disembark at South Bank and walk up the street ramp. I lean against a fence and scan all the people on both platforms for anybody who might be Errol, or Lindsey.

After the station I walk through the park and spot two Aboriginal men and one woman sitting beneath a tree. From his size and the way he's sitting I think one of the men might be Errol. I feel like the new vulture. I try not to gawk. As I get closer I realise they're both too young. The men ignore me and I keep my mouth closed. I don't have the guts to ask 'Do any of you know a bloke called Errol?'

I sit waiting on a park bench and hope I'm not pegged for a pervert. I scan each new arrival but when none are my brothers I give up and walk towards the river and Brisbane's Cultural Precinct.

A life-size pregnant southern right whale and her juvenile calf hang moaning in the passageway outside the entrance to the Queensland Museum. The actual whale recordings of moans, clicks and grunts fill the passageway. Like sea anemones, a class of young primary school children in maroon uniforms have stretched up their arms in a futile effort to reach the whales' undersides.

'Line up. Line up!' a young teacher commands in a frazzle.

This is the museum that used to be located north side but was moved when the south bank became Brisbane's cultural marshalling yard. Just in from the museum's front doors small animal footprints lead me to words stencilled on a wall.

DISCOVER QUEENSLAND
THE INSIDE GUIDE TO THE STATE OUTSIDE
VISIT AMAZING PLACES!
MEET WONDERFUL PEOPLE!
HEAR FASCINATING STORIES!
BEGIN A LIFETIME'S JOURNEY OF DISCOVERY!
ROUGH ROAD

And there, past the gibbers and the shingle-back lizards, locked behind glass, is the object I remember most from childhood visits: a riveted black metal container, warped and empty, with holes in its bottom and sides.

The tank was originally a ship's water tank used by the Watsons as a cauldron in which to boil sea cucumbers to produce trepang. The oars were paddles used to stir the trepang during cooking. Holes were chopped in its sides and bottom to drain out the water before Mrs Watson's body was removed.

'Stay in your groups,' the panicking young teacher calls, leading her charges into the exhibit. 'Stay in your groups.'

I remember as a child being introduced to Mrs Watson's tank on a visit from my own primary school. Errol was in my grade but in a different class. He was shy and before the bus trip Mum took me aside and asked me to keep him company. Mum needn't have worried because I could see Errol talking and laughing, making fish swimming movements with his hands as he described where he came from to the boy sitting next to him.

'Stay in your groups.'

Moving in two lines between shelves full of dusty old insects, clothes and rocks, none of us paid too much attention to the things about us until we happened upon a strange dull black metal container.

The teacher clapped her hands.

'This lady is Mrs Watson,' the teacher said, pointing to a photo of a lady in old-fashioned clothes.

'And this is Mrs Watson's tank,' she said, indicating the black metal container.

'Nearly a hundred years ago Mrs Watson moved to Queensland from Scotland.' The teacher said.

The photo of the woman reminded me of pictures of the Tsarina.

'This lady married Mr Watson and they had a baby boy. They lived on Lizard Island with their two faithful Chinese servants.'

She stopped speaking to listen for complete silence.

'Mr Watson went away to work.' The teacher peered at the plaque. 'To collect sea cucumbers.'

I imagined the cucumber sandwiches that royal people like to eat morning, noon and night and I realised the importance of knowing as much about them as I could in case I was ever quizzed at a fancy ball or State occasion: 'These are delicious David, what are they? You must give me the recipe!'

'Cucumber sandwiches,' I imagined myself saying. 'They grow in the sea.'

The teacher's voice pierced my fantasy.

'Aborigines attacked the house and one of the two servants vanished.'

'What happened to the servant who disappeared?' Errol's friend asked quietly.

The teacher, delighted with everyone's attention, made a dead engine noise and drew a line across her throat.

'The Aborigines scared poor Mrs Watson so much that she and the remaining servant pushed this black cauldron into the water, got in with the baby, and floated away.'

Thirty pairs of eyes now focus on the interior of the black tank imagining a lady, her baby and a Chinese man.

'They floated for days and days before beaching on a deserted and waterless island. Just imagine the poor baby's desperate cries.'

'The Chinese man went and lay down under a tree. We know this because Mrs Watson wrote down everything in her diary.' The teacher pointed at an open book lined in old black leather. 'Rain finally fell after the three of them had died and the men who found them had to chop holes in the bottoms and sides,' the teacher indicated with a finger the slices and holes in the black metal, 'to drain out the water. Then they removed the bodies of Mrs Watson and her baby.'

The black container in front of us held the dead bodies of a mother and child. The black box is an open coffin. A girl from my class burst into tears and her sobs set off a few of the others.

On the way home in the bus Errol and his friend weren't talking.

I realised the reason why Errol, Lindsey and their sister were taken off their parents. It must have been as punishment for Mrs Watson and her baby.

But now, here in the 21ˢᵗ century, there is no mention of the most gruesome bit, the dead baby. I reread the tagline. The baby boy has been removed from the story of Mrs Watson's tank. But even without the child the weight of the tank is immense. It was from this cauldron, different to the football stadium called the Cauldron, that lots of kids were ladled out their first taste of white/black relations.

Looking round I can't locate anything to counterbalance the weight of this black tank. There's space given over to giant cockroaches, the Queensland Lungfish, and the butterfly man of Kuranda. There's an explanation of what happened to Aboriginal pathways: *Most modern towns and settlements are built on important Aboriginal sites and many roads follow the traditional trade routes.* The closest approximation is the taking of sugar slaves from the South Pacific.

There is no corresponding Aboriginal Mrs Watson and her tank, and her baby — nothing of that immediacy and power to put viewers in a black mother's shoes. There still isn't any context. The tank needs to be accompanied at all times by a warden to explain the danger, or at least a corresponding installation, a hologram, reversing the colours: a white tank and a black Mrs Watson.

The display right next to Mrs Watson's tank is on trepang processing. A withered sea cucumber is tethered to the wall. The sea cucumber is animal, not vegetable, and I can't imagine its flesh in a sandwich.

Are You My Mother?

'Good morning 9C.'

'Good morning Mr Benson.'

'I want to introduce you to your new physical education teacher.'

The woman standing with the Head of the P.E. Department is stocky like a shot-put champion.

'Miss Fisher comes to us well prepared, having taught at several different high schools, so don't think you'll be able to put anything over her. Am I right Miss Fisher?'

'Right you are Mr Benson. Now I want the class on the ground and showing me twenty push-ups each.'

School bags are shucked to the earth and groans and dust fill the air as we fall to our knees.

Miss Fisher. My mother. This is it. I remember the name on my hospital bracelet written in my mother's diary.

I've read about this phenomenon in *Women's Weekly* magazine where adopted people's real parents often live on the periphery of their children's lives without either party knowing until much later. The article supplied two examples: a girl who used to borrow books from the library where her birth mother was librarian; and a woman who for years had her groceries packed by the son she'd given up long ago.

Each lunch hour now finds me loitering at the sporting equipment sheds trying to engage Miss Fisher in conversation as to her movements since 1965. To be my mother she needs to be 27 years old.

'If you don't mind me asking, how long does it take to be a P.E. teacher?'

'Three years.'

'Did you go straight into university after school?'

'Yes.'

'You don't look very old to be a teacher.'

'I'll take that as a compliment. I'm twenty-seven.'

'Ahhhhh.'

'Look, it's not really my place but you're obviously here for a reason that has nothing to do with physical education. Am I right?'

This is developing too quickly . . . I'm not ready. This woman is my birth mother. I can't speak. I just nod my head.

'You're hanging about because you know what I am.'

I am teetering on the edge of something momentous. If I talk I will fall in a heap. I can only nod again.

'I know it's horrible and lonely, but it's a different world once you've left school. You'll find acceptance and friends who will understand and love you.'

I'm getting the feeling we are talking about two different things. I'm waiting for her to open her arms but instead she is talking about the world outside.

'I remember being your age and too frightened to tell anyone about how I was feeling.'

Oh, she must be talking about how scared she was being young and pregnant, but I'm male and it doesn't have any bearing unless she is trying to say sorry for giving me up.

'Being a homosexual is nothing to be ashamed of.'

My mother is a homosexual?

No. Miss Fisher thinks I am. She can tell just by looking at me. She's not my mother.

I flee from the sport sheds and drop physical education classes for community service where I go to old people's homes and listen to their stories about the good old days.

Meat and Three Veg

I accompany Beth to the pub she works at in Fortitude Valley. The car radio is tuned to a local station and the rant is about the second match of the State of Origin series, and how New South Wales doesn't stand a chance.

'God, I hope the Maroons lose!'

'You should support Queensland at State of Origin,' Beth says, looking sideways at me. 'It's the only time Queensland supports its black fellas!'

'Jesus, Beth, I don't know how you can live up here after everything that happened.'

'I love Queensland,' she says simply. 'Bloody hell, David, even the Jews moved back to Germany! What's your problem? All you got was a few clips about the ear.'

'No, that's not all!' I exclaim, twisting about in my seat, 'and it's not all about Ron. I moved away because Queensland passed a law where gays, deviants and perverts in those days – thank you – couldn't even have a drink together in a pub. I was strip searched on the side of the road for Christ's sake. Twice!'

'Well, yeah, that's horrible – but Nelson Mandela still lives in South Africa doesn't he?'

'Yeah, but I bet he doesn't go so far as to barrack for their football team.'

'Yeah he does,' Beth replies simply, knowing all about football.

'Well, I'm not,' I declare.

After parking in the spaces assigned to staff, Beth shows me round the Ye Olde English pub. She tells me the pub has always had a large Aboriginal clientele. I'm surprised anyone, let alone Aboriginal people, would want to hang about in a Ye Olde English pub but I'm still smarting from our conversation in the car so I keep my criticisms to myself.

The tour ends out the back in the staff smoking area where Beth leaves me with a beer while she changes a patron's money for the poker machines. There's a wall of photographs in the staff section of all the people barred from entering the hotel for one reason or another. Someone has written WALL OF SHAME in black felt tip pen above the images. Half of the pictures are of Aboriginal people caught by security cameras in the act of begging, stealing or soliciting. The other half are either hungry European backpackers or old, tantrum-throwing white men.

Beth comes up behind me and stabs the tip of her index fingernail firmly into the photographed face of a 50-year-old white man.

'That guy there is a convicted rapist,' she says. 'I told management I caught him stealing so I don't ever have to serve him.'

'What? He wasn't caught stealing?'

'Nope, I'm not serving rapists. The ones I know about anyway.'

'Beth's Liquor Act 2007,' I say, in awe.

My sister has to go and balance the tills so I give her a kiss and walk into the city. There's an Aboriginal man fronting a country and western band in the Queen Street Mall. As he sings he sticks out his tongue between the words. I watch for a while remembering how Errol used to drum his fingers on any hard surface available. I continue walking, looking for other Aboriginal men – looking at them for too long when I find them.

The City of Brisbane now has a Tiffany's store with a huge African American security guard at the front door.

How sophisticated, I say to myself, but the sarcasm is hollow. Things have changed. The city is rich and looks good. I'm grudging in my admiration of the place. Brisbane has moved on but I'm stuck in the past.

I walk to the river and look across to the Cultural Precinct. The colour of the stone makes the buildings look like a continuation of the Kangaroo Point cliffs downstream. The architecture looks just as immovable, as if it could exist for thousands of years. The style is reminiscent of another building, one I can't quite recall.

Falling in with students from all over the world I cross the bridge to get to the library. Off to the left I catch sight of the tall parliamentary building caught up in the green and white coils of the riverside expressway. *Strangle snake, strangle. Strangle till it pops.* This is the building where the law that sent me packing had been made. It's a strange comfort to know I can't let go of old hurts.

Up close the Queensland State Library looks like the shorn-off trunk of a Moreton Bay Fig tree. People move like insects between moss-coloured buttresses. It is cool and beautiful.

In the foyer a notice advertises an exhibition on the third level about Queensland's stolen generations. It's an omen. Below the standard numbers on the lift buttons are raised dots, nearly invisible, like insect eggs, and it takes a second to realise its Braille.

Wow, I sneer to myself, *my home State has really turned considerate in its old age.*

Upstairs I walk in on a short silent film running on a loop. It contains images of early Cherbourg: footage of a school building looking similar in style to any suburban school building; two white nurses staffing a hospital, and admiring footage of Aboriginal children being taught woodcraft and home economics; a team of Aboriginal men in the 1930s building a bridge and driving a car over it.

This is what I have to do. Build a bridge and get over it or I'll be trapped in my self-indulgent whingeing forever. Once the film loops the loop, I go to a computer and punch in the words, Cherbourg, Queensland.

A couple of books are listed. I locate the most recent one on the shelves and scan its index for any mention of my brother's last name. Nothing. I start at the beginning and read the foreword where the author thanks the elders of Cherbourg for the trust they've shown in him. The author thanks the Rabato family. A instead of an E: one letter difference. Is this family related to Errol but time has changed the spelling? I wonder, if I contact the author, will he put me in touch?

Waiting for takeaway coffee in the library café and bookshop, I flick through coffee table books and read that the Brisbane River is older than the Nile.

The Brisbane River is older than the Nile. How can that be?

I know the names of ancient Egyptian rulers – male and female. I know of Ra, and sun worship, Tutankhamen and Nefertiti. I know more about Ancient Egyptians who lived along the Nile than I know about the people who once walked the earth beneath the bookshop café.

And then I remember the building whose style the cultural centre reminded me of when I stood looking from the other side of the river. The Temple of Hatshepsut. Pictures from the library books my eyes searched as a child looking for the place where I imagined the evil queen drowned in sand. The same flat roof and same colour stone, similar terraces and colonnades, as if the Temple of Hatshepsut had been picked up out of the Valley of Kings and plonked down here. As if the brown Brisbane River were the new River Nile.

A small group of Aboriginal people is gathered round a bonfire in Musgrave Park. It's the biggest group I've seen but none of the men are my brothers. Some of their children are playing on the swings and a line of private school kids are trudging single file with their heads down through the park like wildebeest on the Kalahari. Soft rain starts to fall as I head back towards Vulture St.

After a few drinks that night I lift my hand in Beth's direction for the cigarette lighter and she pretends to flinch. It's supposed to be a joke about the time I hit her when I was 12. I still remember it. SLAP, SLAP, SLAP, SLAP, SLAP, SLAP, SLAP: three times on each side of her face, and one for good measure, just because she wasn't playing a game the way I wanted it played. I remember the obscene rush of power. Beth says she couldn't believe her brother she loved so much was hitting her. Our relationship changed. She was eight.

But that's not all.

'Can't you make any white friends?' I asked casually, when she wouldn't come back to revering me the old way. Her best friend in those days was a girl with an Afro who'd moved here from the Solomon Islands.

Beth has never mentioned this, so I don't think she remembers. I put her memory failure down to all the pot she smokes. Marijuana does have fringe benefits for me after all.

But she remembers the hitting.

When Beth flinches I'm supposed to laugh. It's a joke. Then I apologise all over again. I beg her to hit my face as hard as she can, 10 times, three more for luck, and never mention it again, but she won't – she says she likes to see me squirm. This is my cue to arrange to stay somewhere else. We're getting on each other's nerves.

'Tomorrow, after I've done a bit more searching, I'll go and stay somewhere else for the night. Give you a break.'

The next morning I ring my mother's sister and ask if I can stay. I give her my arrival details and offer to make dinner as a thank-you.

Thirty minutes later I again disembark at the old Vulture Street train station and head towards Musgrave Park. Except for a schoolgirl in uniform sitting against a wall of the swimming centre there's no one else about. It dawns on me that Errol could be at work like everybody else. I'm suddenly embarrassed that I've subscribed to this stereotype of Errol still being footloose and fancy-free.

I promised to make dinner for my aunt and uncle and I'm suddenly worried about the availability of ingredients. I leave the park and cross the river into the city. I find an inner-city supermarket and ask the girl attending to the meat slicer whether the chorizo sausage on display is available in all suburban Queensland outlets.

'Chorizo is available everywhere sir,' she answers, keeping her eyes on the meat curls falling onto her plastic gloved hand. 'It's a pretty standard product.'

Of course it is. What am I thinking? Why do I still think Brisbane is stuck in a past of meat and three veg? Watching the meat drop from the machine I recognise I've been sliced in three. The first slice is the little kid in the tree; the middle is me from the eighties; and the last is me now. They alternate who's in control. Eighties me is the version doing the food shopping, unaware it's no longer 1985.

My aunt is out front of the train station in her car and we head towards her place. I tell her I'm looking for Errol. She asks, 'How do you know he's still alive?'

I tell her the story of ringing the Cherbourg police and how the officer knew Errol had just left town to travel back to Brisbane.

'Maybe he's on parole and that's why they know so much about him.'

I hadn't thought of this and I wonder what he could have done. I hope it wasn't violent. I hope it wasn't rape.

My aunt stops to negotiate a roundabout where a gang of council workers are digging up a bed of small burgundy-coloured hedges.

'They're digging up all that prissy, exotic nandina and replacing them with xanthorrhoea.' She motions to a freshly laid bed of Australian natives. 'I refuse to call them blackboys.'

My aunt tells me how, over the years, they've searched the electoral rolls and rung the few listings under Rebato but never found anything. My aunt asks me why I'm not looking for Lindsey first as he was my brother for the longest.

I say my feelings about Lindsey are more complicated.

I recount the article I found in the newspaper and read to Mum on her deathbed. How a man called Lindsey Rebato had been arrested impersonating a police officer and extorting money from men frequenting toilet blocks.

My aunt raises an eyebrow and gives me an appraising look.

'I don't hang around toilet blocks,' I say, in a bored voice. 'Lindsey's behaviour suggests he has a problem with men who have sex with men. That he's the moral police with benefits.'

'Well,' she says, 'I've got a problem with men who have sex in toilet blocks!'

'Yes, but you're not going to pretend to be a policeman and blackmail money off them are you.'

Just at that moment the car passes parkland and a squat toilet block comes into view.

'Shall I pull over?' my Aunt asks.

'Ha, ha,' I say, with a flick of my hand. 'When we were teenagers Lindsey told me to turn to Christ when he heard I was gay. Dad did too.'

'What did your mother do?'

'She burst into tears.'

'Well I guess it must have come as a shock.'

'Oh, yeah, a shock. She took me to a psychiatrist when I was 10. Anyway, I read the article about Lindsey to Mum, and we had a discussion about contacting the police station for information about him but we both knew I wouldn't. It was the wrong time.'

My aunt keeps driving but stays silent.

'What if he'd been completely crazy?' I say. 'Mum was dying and we were all bloody exhausted.'

'But now you feel you had the chance to take him to her for his sake, like a real brother would,' she indicates, turning into her street, 'so he could say goodbye, and you didn't.'

'Yeah.'

Looking resolutely out the window I'm ashamed all over again. I remember magpie season, being six years old, and walking to school wearing an ice-cream container over my head. I looked like a little robot. From under the plastic rim I could just see enough of Lindsey's legs and feet to keep on track. Lindsey wasn't wearing a helmet of any kind but was carrying a stick to ward the attacking birds away. I can still remember the smell of vanilla and the pale light seeping in through the plastic walls, and I remember knowing I could follow Lindsey anywhere because he would never lead me astray.

The supermarket a kilometre from my aunt's place has more chorizo sausages than I've seen in all Newcastle's shops combined. That night I make my thank-you dinner: pasta combined with chorizo, Spanish onion, roast pumpkin and baby rocket, but my aunt doesn't seem too impressed and neither does my uncle.

Spelling

The following morning I ring the author of the Cherbourg book and rush through my spiel.

'My name is David and I'm trying to locate my Aboriginal foster brother whose last known address was in Cherbourg.'

'So what can I do?'

'In the foreword you thank the elders for their stories and go on to say that without their help you wouldn't have gotten anywhere. I'm hoping you can put me in touch with the same people.'

'Ring Bev Johnson. She's a community officer in Cherbourg and knows everyone.' I can hear him turning pages of an address book: 'Got a pen?'

I copy down the number, thank him, and hang up the phone. My heart is beating fast. I feel 10 steps closer to finding Errol. I dial the number.

'Welfare, how can I help?'

'Is Bev Johnson there please?'

'No, Bev's off at a council meeting. She'll be back later on.'

After an hour spent pacing, I ring again, and I'm about to be transferred to the Council department when a woman picks up and says, 'You want to speak with Aunty Bev?'

'Yes.'

I am forwarded to another area.

'Hello, can I help you?' A no-nonsense voice.

'Bev Johnson?'

'Yes.'

I explain my contact with the author, and my search for my foster brother.

'He used to live in Cherbourg and maybe still does.'

'You're his brother?'

'Yeah, I'm his brother. I haven't seen him for 20 years.' I wonder if she heard the word foster and discarded it as unimportant.

I wait for Bev Johnson to ask 'Brother? How can you prove you're his brother? What sort of brother waits all this time? Are you white?'

'Yes,' I would have to say, 'Yes I am white.'

'Does he have blue eyes?' she asks.

The question throws me. Blue eyes in an Aboriginal face. Surely I would remember, but no matter how hard I squint into memory I can't distinguish Errol's eye colouring. I want to say green, but I'm scared of giving the wrong answer.

'No, I think greeny brown.'

'Where are you ringing from?' Her voice is kind.

'Brisbane, but I live in Newcastle. I'm only in town a little while.'

'Wait one minute.'

I hear her put the phone down and ask other people who must be in the same room whether anyone knows Errol. I hear a woman say 'Yes' but her tone is non-committal, flat. I can't pick from this woman's voice whether knowing him is a good thing or a bad thing. Other words, murmured words, flit through the holes of the receiver unrecognised.

Bev returns to the phone.

'No one's seen him for a long time. (*But the police said he'd just left. Someone must be wrong.*) He lived round the Aspley area, but that's a while ago now and he might have moved. Have you tried Musgrave Park and asking there?'

'I've been to the park, but I didn't find anything.' I'm silently thrilled this has been a valid option all along. 'I thought that might be rude to just front up asking questions.'

'Everyone's looking for someone,' she says.

I'm confused. I can't tell whether she thinks all whites are looking for someone or if she thinks I'm an Aboriginal person trying to locate lost family members. I don't want to deceive this woman. Then I wonder why I'm thinking like this. I am white and I am looking for someone. And maybe Bev is right. Maybe everyone, black and white, is looking for someone.

'I'm going to put you through to Roberta in rehab. She'll know more about him, okay?'

'Thank you very much.' The word rehab rings in my ear. Does this mean Errol was committed?

Somewhere in Cherbourg a phone rings.

'Rehab, Roberta speaking.'

I tell Roberta the story I told Bev – that I'm Errol's foster brother looking for him after 20 years.

'Have you been to Musgrave Park?'

Roberta sounds younger than Bev.

'Yes, but I couldn't find him and I thought it was rude to ask.'

'Everyone's looking for someone,' she sighs, and I wonder if this is Cherbourg's motto. 'Errol has a sister living in Brisbane called Yvonne.'

'I didn't know about Yvonne,' I reply, surprised, remembering the little girl who came to our house. 'I knew about Sasha. I met her.'

I feel stupid that I haven't allowed for the existence of other sisters. Roberta and Bev must have deduced I'm white or else how does it explain why Errol has a sister called Yvonne that I don't know about? Unless the stealing was like a production line: give birth – taken/give birth – taken/give birth – taken.

'Look in the phone book. Yvonne spells her last name differently. Yvonne's is spelt Rabato and she lives in Woodridge.'

I thank Roberta, hang up, and flump open the phone book.

Rabato, Y 63 Cuthbert St, Woodridge (07) 36540000

Lindsey and Errol's sister. So this is it. So simple.

My heart is beating fast and steady.

'Hello,' a soft voice, 'Yvonne speaking.'

I introduce myself and tell her that I'm looking for Errol Rebato – my foster brother. I explain I've already rung Cherbourg and spoken with Bev Johnson and Roberta in rehab.

'I know Errol.'

Her voice is air-conditioner cool and the skin along my arms prickles into a forest of tiny igloos. Present tense. Errol is alive.

'Where did you grow up?' Her voice remains soft but now has a business-like tone.

'Ipswich, then after Mum left Dad, Bayside, where Errol and Lindsey ran away.'

I can sense Yvonne ticking off my story with what she knows of Errol's upbringing. I can tell I add up. I ask her if she knows anything of Lindsey.

'Last I heard he was in a psych ward on the Gold Coast.'

I tell Yvonne that I had no idea she existed. I say I knew a girl called Sasha, but I'd never heard of an Yvonne. I prattle on and on. I ask if she is in touch with Sasha and recount the story of meeting her in the backyard of our house years before.

'She's dead.' She waits a heartbeat. 'I'll get you Errol's number and address.'

Sasha, the little girl who went on a hunger strike to meet her brothers, is dead. Sasha, the little girl who could have ended up in our family. If Sasha had come into our family she would have met Ron. I can't wish that on anyone. Rayley, the girl who took Sasha's place in our family, is also dead. She died of heart disease at thirty.

'Are you there?' Yvonne asks into the phone. 'This is Errol's mobile number.'

It never occurred to me Errol would have a mobile phone. The *Crocodile Dundee* movie springs to mind where an Aboriginal man wearing a loincloth and covered in tribal paint markings makes an incongruous sight gag by pulling out his mobile phone. I'm alarmed. Subconsciously I've been subscribing to the same joke.

Yvonne reels off the digits, and there in front of me is my brother's phone number.

Yvonne says Errol lives by himself in a north side suburb called Aspley. She tells me Errol's at work at this time of the day, that it's best to leave a message.

Errol's at work.

I've been staring at Aboriginal men at the park and in malls and Errol's been working all along.

'Thank you so much, and it's good to finally speak with you.'

'Finally?' she says with a guffaw. 'You didn't know I existed till today.'

'No,' I reply awkwardly, not able to think much beyond Errol's phone number, 'thanks anyway.'

'It's a pleasure.'

I gather my belongings and return to the train station for the trip back to Beth's. I will ring from there. Scared I will lose his number I hold the paper in my hand. Then, in the final minutes of the journey, I'm fearful the moisture from my hand will melt the numbers away. While the train whines on, I tear a notebook page into pieces. I copy down his number over and over again, *quickly, before the train derails in a flaming heap, or a bomb explodes,* then I hide each folded piece away in different pockets and separate areas of my bag and wallet till I'm satisfied nothing will ever again make me lose his contact details.

I ring six times from Beth's house but each time the number rings out and fails to divert to message bank. I worry that the number is obsolete, or wrong, that Yvonne heard something she didn't like in my voice, something false, and has deliberately given me the wrong number.

Beth arrives home after her shift and we share a cigarette on the back porch while I tell her about the failed phone calls. Beth wants to see the number on the piece of paper for herself. I'm explaining my frustration at not knowing whether there's something wrong with Errol's phone, or the number, when the landline I've been trying to leave messages from starts to ring.

'No one dials that number,' Beth whispers hoarsely. 'People ring my mobile.'

It can't be anyone else. Beth steps away for me to answer it. I pick up.

'Hello?'

'Yep?'

'Hello?'

'Why have you been ringing me?'

The voice is equal-parts man and nicotine.

'Errol?'

'Yep.'

Ants erupt from holes in my skin.

'It's David.' I want to add 'your brother' but I stop.

'David who?'

'David, your . . . ' I can't . . . I need him to say it first. 'We grew up together.'

'My foster brother, David?'

HE SAYS IT HE SAYS IT HE SAYS IT

'Yeah, David. Your brother.'

'Are you for real? Are you for real?'

Beth stands with one hand over her mouth, and with the other starts making fast upwards and downwards movements as if it's a pump to reverse the water racing to the edges of her saucer eyes.

'Yeah, Blackstone Road. Mungala Street. Peel Street.' I reel off our childhood addresses like I'm showing off passport stamps.

'What are you ringing me for?' he says soberly.

His abruptness throws me. I thought it was obvious.

'Because I wanted to find you,' I say, deciding quickly against adding the caveat, 'I'm writing about this, about you and me and where we've ended up.'

'I didn't think anybody was interested in what happened to me.' There's a tone of disbelief in his voice. 'How did you find me?'

'I rang Cherbourg and spoke with Bev Johnson and Roberta in rehab and they put me onto your sister Yvonne and she gave me your number.'

I also fail to mention the police station.

Errol is chuckling at the process involved.

'I didn't think anyone was interested,' he repeats.

'Where are you now?' I ask.

'At work, I left my phone in my locker and I found these six missed calls. Where are you?'

'At Beth's.' I turn back and look at her and she's given up trying not to cry and her eyes and cheeks are soaking wet and she has the biggest grin. 'Do you remember Beth?'

'My sister?' His voice takes off in another flying leap. 'Yeah of course! Hey, where do you live?'

'Newcastle.'

'Why do you want to live down there?' His voice wheels about suspiciously.

'I go to university down there.' I decide not to tell him about Jason, or of my feelings for my home state.

'How's Mum?'

Oh God.

'Mum died.'

'When?' His voice bogs.

'Ten years ago.' I feel the insult in the words, and their implica-
tion — *why didn't you find me then?*

'We looked,' I say weakly, 'but no one could find you.'

'Who did?'

'Me. Every time I came to Brisbane I scanned the streets. And
Aunty Anne and Uncle Wayne checked the electoral rolls and rang
all listings in the phone book, but your sister spells her last name
differently.'

Excuses, excuses, excuses.

I remember how Mum's will failed to mention the foster kids as
if they didn't exist.

To get away from the unpleasantness I hustle him to the next
window of his life as if he's a spectator.

'Ron died,' I offer as recompense, 'a horrible death from cancer.'

'He got his karma,' Errol speaks low and I can barely hear him,
'for all the bad things he did.'

'Mum died of cancer too,' I interject, 'but at least she had all her
kids round her.'

It's out of my mouth before I can stop it. Not all of us were there
at all. Errol wasn't, neither was Lindsey or Rayley, and I can't vouch
that Ron's boys weren't gathered about his dying body either.

'Have you got a woman,' he changes gears, 'or any kids?'

'No.' I throw a look of horror at Beth, and laugh awkwardly.
Surely he must remember the eyeliner I was wearing the last time
he saw me in King George Square.

'No, I don't have kids, or a woman.'

Beth is stifling laughter and I shush her with a hand movement.

'Do you have a wife,' I turn it round, 'or a girlfriend, or any kids?'

'No wife. But I've got a boy up in Cherbourg,' Errol chuckles quietly. 'He's angry at me because I can't afford to buy him football boots.'

'Karen is married and has four boys.'

'Karen, hey?' His voice swells with pride. 'She's doing well.'

'Have you seen Lindsey?' I ask.

'Not for years. I heard he was in a psych hospital.'

I don't know what to say to this so I just continue through the roll call.

'Did you find your real mother and father?'

'I met my mother on her death bed in Cherbourg, and my father lives up on Palm Island. Hey, the last time I saw Lindsey I tried to tell him about our family on Palm but he wasn't interested.'

I silently thank God Errol was at the deathbed of his real mother – and then realise how fucked up this is. I also remember the three brothers who'd been killed in the car accident but decide not to mention them.

'Hey, I'm sorry your mother died.'

'Yeah,' he's quiet for a second, 'both of em.'

'Have you been up to Palm Island?'

'Yep, I was up there a while back.'

'Did you know Doomadgee?' God, why can't I think of anything *happy* to say?

'Yeah, he was a good bloke. A joker. He didn't deserve that.'

'Don't worry about it. That cop will get his,' I say like I know, 'Queensland's changed.'

'When can I see you?' he asks brusquely, moving me away from things I know nothing about.

'Yeah, when? We can't this afternoon because we're going to see Dad,' and then I qualify, 'the bloke that fostered you and adopted me.'

'He still alive?'

'Yeah, he's still alive and married to his fourth wife! He's had two since Mum.'

'That's my Dad!' he bellows.

'How about tomorrow?'

Beth shouts, 'I'll drive!'

'I finish work at quarter past two and I'm home by 2:30.'

'We'll be there on the dot!' I write Errol's address beneath his telephone number and underline it. I can't think of anything else to say. We say goodbye and hang up.

The receiver is barely back in its cradle when Beth grabs my arm and we're both hopping up and down on the spot screaming and laughing.

'We found Errol! We found Errol!'

'No.' Beth pulls me into her version of a bear hug. 'You found Errol and I'm so proud of you.'

Father Figure

Our Dad, the man Mum left 30 years ago, has hair like a mad scientist in a black and white movie, but his eyes are the crispest blue.

'Guess what Dad,' I yell through the flyscreen as he shuffles to unlock the door. 'We found Errol!'

Because of his multiple strokes Dad moves slowly and his left arm hangs uselessly at his side.

'Oh, yeah?' Dad says in a high old man voice. 'How is he?'

'He's really good. He lives in Aspley.'

'Yeah?' Noncommittal, like I'm blithely telling him gossip about someone he doesn't know. I don't expect him to break out in a song or a dance, but I do want more from him than just *Yeah?* I want Dad to say he can't wait to see him, but he doesn't.

Gwen, Dad's fourth wife, bustles out from the kitchen and gives Beth and me a hug. Our mother was Dad's second wife. His first wife divorced him for reasons lost in time. Dad's third wife committed suicide the day he retired. She had a disease called lupus. He found her laid out on the duvet in the bedroom with a plastic bag over her head when he came in from work. She'd tied it shut with a red ribbon like it was a present. A woman down the road told Dad that his wife had told her she couldn't bear the thought of him being underfoot all day everyday adding to her pain.

Dad knew the thought of his constant presence had been worrying her and had lined up a part-time mowing job at an old people's home but the drought broke and it rained and rained. The grass grew and the administrators couldn't wait the few days for him to finish work, so hired someone else. That's when she did it.

'Someone's always out to cut my grass,' he sighed at the funeral.

We'd invited Dad to Mum's last Christmas on Earth. He didn't leave the side of her hospital cot. He held her hand and cried and told her he never stopped loving her. I couldn't tell if Mum understood, or even cared.

Dad returns to his recliner and sits staring out the window at the electricity lines and Gwen takes over the conversation.

'Your father is going in for an endoscopy at the end of the month.'

Medical item number 11820. One of the numbers I remember off by heart.

'He's been waiting six months to get into the hospital system. I told him we should have private health insurance but he doesn't listen.'

'Six months,' he nods, turning away from the electricity wires, 'but I'm still not looking forward to it.'

'His doctor thinks he's bleeding internally.'

We don't stay long. As we get into the car Beth says that we should go to Karen's and get Mum's old photos. She says there might be some of Errol we can show when we visit him. I wish I had the one of the three of us standing on the log tower at Bullen's African Lion Safari. It would help me to explain to Errol that I'm gay.

'Look,' I'd say, pointing to my limp hands hanging in front of me, 'it was obvious.'

Boomerang

'Wow,' is all Karen can say when we tell her about finding Errol. She makes us sit down and tell it from the beginning.

'Does he have any kids?'

'One,' I repeat, 'a boy. But Errol says he can't afford his football boots.'

Karen's brow creases slightly but she doesn't say anything. I wonder why it's this bit of information I chose to relay. And then I realise. I'm using Karen as a miner uses a canary to warn of poisonous gas. I'm scared Errol will ask for what he is owed. But surely if he's my brother he's entitled.

Beth grabs Mum's remaining photos and Karen's parting words are for us to be careful, as we don't know what time or circumstance has done to Errol.

I scoff and tell her not to be silly, and hug her again.

As Beth drives I flick through the photos and find one of Errol in a football jersey standing against a backdrop of scarred and bruised banana trunks.

The next afternoon I ring Errol on Beth's mobile and say we are pulling into a drive-through bottle shop and ask whether there's anything he'd like us to bring.

'I don't drink during the week but don't let that stop you.'

The thing to do would be for Beth to drive right through without stopping. If Errol doesn't drink alcohol during the week we should honour this and not take alcohol into his house. Like a breeze through curtains, everything I've read about booze and Aboriginal men flutters through my head, but I shut the window.

'It's a celebration,' I tell myself, knowing the beer will be there primarily to calm my nerves.

'A case of XXXX please,' I say to the car attendant.

We drive north over the Story Bridge and through the old north-side trinity of museum, hospital and showground. The old museum building with its towers and cupolas is still standing. I think about Mrs Watson's tank. I imagine the ghost of Mrs Watson staring mournfully at us from the top of one of the museum towers.

Past the old museum is the Royal Women's Hospital and I wonder how my birth mother had arrived that day. Whether, with me in her belly, she caught a cab, an ambulance, or in those days maybe even a tram. I bet, whichever way, she was scared.

Twenty minutes later we pull up in front of a long, thin strand of flats.

A man wearing a shirt of bright orange reflector panels sewn onto a dark background stands looking out an open window. His stance looks uncertain. It may be the shadows in the room but his skin looks smoky. There is a faint discolouration about his mouth like he's a Papuan who chews betel nut. The man looks old. I don't recognise him. We've found the wrong man.

'Errol didn't mention a flatmate,' I say. There is an Aboriginal flag in the window and a boomerang leaning against the windowpane. It must be him. He was always proud.

'I'll just bring in one six-pack,' I whisper.

We step out and open the trunk of the car. I rip open the cardboard flaps and remove the beer. We head towards the small flight of stairs that takes us to a corridor that leads to the flat's front door. I'm on the second step when the front door opens. The man from the window is standing there. He is short. Errol was never short: he was always huge. I reach the top of the stairs. The man hasn't shaved and the stubble about his mouth and chin is grey. His eyes are greenie brown and the smile on his lips is not too shy and not a grin.

It's Errol. He puts his hand out and I take it in mine. His hand is small and rough. The top of his head barely reaches my shoulders. I remember the muscle man 20 years ago in King George Square and I wonder what has happened.

'Look at you.' He looks me up and down. 'You got big!'

I want to hug him but I don't. I stumble sideways into his flat. Behind me Beth introduces herself, 'Do you remember me? I'm the little redhead with freckles.'

I turn in time to see her force a hug on him.

The kitchen, dining and lounge are all in one room. A small television with the volume turned low faces a two-seater couch. Judge Judy is in the middle of making one of her pronouncements. A rectangular table, covered in swirling green and blue plastic, is pushed flush beneath the window. Three vinyl chairs have their seats tucked beneath the other three sides. Behind the table and chairs is the kitchen area.

The pantry door is partially open and I can see neat shelves of evenly spaced condiments. A collection of trucker hats hangs off individual pegs on a wall differentiating the living area from the bedroom. Through a second doorway I can see an unmade bed and shoes kicked off under it. I'm spying but I can't help myself.

Errol's flat is as austere as a monk's residence, or a prison cell. I wonder if he'd tidied because we were coming. But surely he wouldn't have lined up his pantry shelves and left the bed unmade. Making the bed is the first thing a person would do.

I'm still carrying the beer and plastic bag holding the photos. We go and stand by the table. Beth sits with her back to Judge Judy, and I sit in the middle facing the window. Errol goes back to the seat from where he must have risen when we pulled up.

'This is where the king sits!'

It's a joke and he flexes his arm muscles to prove it. I notice he has an outline of Queensland tattooed on his right forearm. After everything that has happened he's still proud of his origins. I angle out a bottle from the pack, open it, hand it to Beth and repeat. There is a half-full ashtray in the middle of the table. I light a cigarette and so does Beth. Errol grabs the remaining beers, twists round in his seat and puts them on the top shelf in the fridge. I don't see much of anything in there. On top of the fridge is a framed picture of a man and a boy. I don't recognise them, but why would I?

'Because it's a special occasion, I'm going to have one too,' Errol says with the door still open. He removes a beer from the door; the four Xs are emblazoned on all our cans.

'Cheers!'

We all take long draughts of beer.

'I can't believe you wanted to find me. I didn't think anybody was interested in what happened to me.'

Errol wants to hear again the process involved in finding him. He sits back. I tell him about punching his name into the computer, how his name comes up within the broader confines of a death in custody case. Errol looks uneasy. I don't mention that I rang the police station. I say that someone I'd spoken to on the phone mentioned they'd seen him in Cherbourg recently. I tell him Beth and I had even been thinking of going to Cherbourg on the pretext of visiting the emu farm to ask about him.

'I haven't been in Cherbourg for two years.' Errol looks for a long time out the window. 'I had to fight those people in Cherbourg, hey. They blamed me for that boy's death. I had to fight over and over.'

'You were just a boy yourself,' I say softly.

'I can't use my fists anymore.' Errol turns his hands over revealing both wrists. 'See these scars? They're from operations I had for carpal tunnel. I'm getting a payout. Should be soon. The company I worked for had me assembling bull bars and putting them on trucks all day. I didn't have mats under my feet or anything,' he mock head-butts the air, 'but I can still fight if I have to.'

'You were the second toughest kid in high school,' I remind him. 'Everybody was more scared of Lindsey.'

'Yeah, but how about this – one time, in a fight down the train station, I was on the ground being kicked in the head by my opponent's friends in the crowd, and I saw Lindsey watching and he didn't do anything.'

'I saw the same fight,' I explain, revealing my own presence. 'I was watching from the train bridge.'

'You were watching?' He can't believe that neither of us stepped in to help.

'I couldn't see anything.' My voice is whiney. 'But I also remember you telling me the last time I saw you at King George Square that Lindsey saved you from a gang of skinheads and then disappeared before you could say thank you.'

'I don't remember that.'

'How can't you remember? That story has remained in my head forever.'

'All the weed and booze fucked my memory. I haven't smoked in two years.'

'I need pot for my back,' Beth says philosophically. 'I ruined my back working in a chicken factory. Pot is the only drug that helps manage the pain.'

'Oh, sister!' Errol's eyes have lit up. 'Don't tell me you've got pot or you'll never get rid of me!'

'Hey, you gave up!' I sound like a wowser so I get up to get another beer from the fridge to prove that I'm not. I rest my eyes on the man in the photograph on the fridge – he's handsome. 'Who're the man and the boy in the photograph?'

'That's me and my son.'

'Really?' The man in the photo is young, sinewy and attractive, with glossy, longish black hair. 'I didn't recognise you. How old is your boy? He looks like a rascal.'

'Thirteen. He lives with his Mum in Cherbourg. I can't afford to buy him his football boots. I will after my payout.'

This is the second time Errol has mentioned his son's football boots. I wonder if I should offer to buy them for him. Before I have the chance Errol pushes his chair roughly back from the table and disappears into his bedroom. We hear him rummaging in a cupboard and then he emerges holding a silver photo album.

'I had a daughter.' He opens the album to a centre page and points to a tiny bundle in a pink blanket. Her eyes are closed. 'She died when she was 12 days old.'

The man holding the tiny baby is the same bloke in the photo on the fridge. It's Errol only because he says it's him. It's as if all the deaths have shrunk and aged him.

'Why did she die?'

'Her mother is a drinker.' Errol's facial muscles faintly quiver. 'I was up on Palm Island visiting my father when I got the call she was dying. That's the first and only time I've ever been on a plane. I had to get smashed to get on.'

Errol walks the album to Beth and shows her the photos of his daughter. She takes the book from him and stares for a long moment.

'What was it like going up to Palm Island for the first time?'

'I had to fight the moment I arrived to prove myself.'

'To prove what?'

'That I wasn't weak. Some of my relatives were jealous I was getting on with Dad so well. The first person I had to fight was my little brother. He's a boxer but I knocked him down.'

I'm reminded of how Lindsey treated Errol when he saw how well Errol was getting on with Mum. How every time Errol coughed up a whack of phlegm as Mum hit his back it was like she'd received a Faberge egg.

'Do you remember when I used to force you all to play the Romanovs?' I say.

Beth shakes her head.

'No,' Errol says. 'What's that?'

'Oh,' I say. 'It was just a game.'

'I remember when we went to pick you up from the orphanage at Nudgee,' I say, to show how good my memory is.

'Hmmm, what do you mean . . . we?' Errol's tone toughens. '*You* had nothing to do with it!'

I'm blushing. 'I mean I was in the car when Mum and Dad went to pick you up.'

'That's more like it.'

'What's your little brother like?'

'He's the only one of us kids that wasn't taken. He's lucky he's been able to live the Aboriginal life. I'm going to buy a boat with my payout and he's going to captain it. There used to be more brothers, but three died in a car crash on their way to Cherbourg for a big family reunion where they were going to meet me for the first time.'

I figure now is as good a time as any to pull out our photos. I place the pile in front of him. Errol gingerly picks up the first photo and then lays it down on the table in front of him. Then he does the same with the next, and the next, as if he's playing Solitaire. He holds each one and asks questions about the people pictured.

'That's us on holiday on Stradbroke Island.' I point out and name each kid.

'That's you, there's me and that's Lindsey.'

There is a lot he doesn't remember. There is one face he's never forgotten. He finds a photo of Mum standing next to Ron and holds it out in front of him like he's going to spit on it.

'I'm going to burn that arsehole.' His voice is venom and he reaches for a lighter.

'Go on,' Beth eggs him, 'burn it.'

'No, don't do that,' my voice panics, 'it's just a photo. Ron's dead and I need all the pictures for my work. So I can remember, even the bad stuff.'

'What work?'

'I write. I want to write about this now.'

'I don't want anybody writing about me,' he says firmly.

I change the subject.

'Mum told me that Ron was gang-raped when he was a little kid,' I say. 'And that's why he was the monster he was.'

'Replicating the worst thing that ever happened to him is no excuse!' Beth says, launching herself violently from her seat.

'I didn't say it was,' I say.

'It sounds like Mum did,' Beth says.

'People naturally try and find reasons for things,' I say, shrugging.

'Yeah, well I don't want to hear them!' Beth says.

'Okay, okay,' I say. 'Sit down and have a drink.'

There is no talking for a few moments as we all take swigs.

'Errol, what happened after you ran away? Where did you go?'

'I slept in train carriages. At night I'd go through bins looking for food.'

'God, how have you survived?' Beth says.

'I've been smoked by a full blood out at Carnarvon Gorge. He wasn't supposed to do it, because he wasn't in his own area, and he had to go off and ask permission from the spirits.'

As he is talking he continues to go through the photos. He

comes to a photo of Jason, Dad and me and looks up questioningly.

'That's Dad, and that's Jason,' I say quietly, pointing at him so there can be no mistake. To qualify I add, 'We've been together for years,' and then I add hopefully, 'you'll really like him.'

For a moment Errol doesn't understand, but then an awkward half smile appears on his face and I can tell he is blushing.

'I thought you knew.' I stumble over my words in my haste. 'I thought you could tell . . . ' I stop myself adding the words, *what I am*, 'from the last time in King George Square. Remember?' I implore him with my hands. 'I was wearing eyeliner, jewellery and had bleached hair.'

'I thought you were punk!'

'Punk?' Beth splutters beer out her nostrils and breaks out into a half-laughing coughing fit. 'Ha, ha, ha. Different P word!'

'Ha, ha, ha, Beth.' Slightly hurt, I throw back, 'like Pothead?'

Errol also bursts into laughter and the strange moment of my having to explain myself is gone.

'I know a couple of blokes like that up on Palmy.' His eyes, more comfortable now, move back to the photo of Jason, and then he levels them back on me. 'They're good blokes. I sometimes drink with them. As long as they don't try anything, they're okay.'

'Wow, gays on Palm. How do they cope?'

'Everybody knows, but nobody talks about it,' Errol says.

'I would have fled to the city,' I say.

'My people call me the uptown nigger,' Errol says, caught in his own thoughts about name-calling, 'because I have my own place and a job and I can look after myself. Back in Cherbourg I almost hung myself a few times. After I did some domestic violence I ran into the bush and tied my neck to a tree, but I realised it wouldn't make a difference to anyone. That's what stopped me. That's why I decided to change and be a good man.'

I want to tell Errol his death would have mattered to me but I say nothing and let him talk.

'There's a lot of shit in that community, hey. Stuff like it's okay to hit your woman if she gets out of line. I hit my sister Yvonne hey.'

'Why?' Beth asks, shifting in her seat.

'She took my meat out of the fridge for dinner when I was saving it for breakfast.'

'Remind me,' Beth says, leaning forward and tapping her cigarette in the ashtray, 'never to touch your food.'

'I wouldn't do that to you sister girl – I wouldn't ever do that to a woman again. That was a long time ago.'

'David hit me,' Beth states it matter-of-factly, 'didn't you David.' It's not a question.

'Yeah,' I say, hating hearing it again, but knowing it will be my due forever, 'a long time ago, and I want you to hit me back and forget about it.'

'Na,' Beth says seriously, 'I prefer to torture you.'

'See this scar here?' Errol hikes up his State of Origin cap. 'A full blood woman black as the night I was sitting in did it with a chair for talking to another woman.' He is chuckling. 'It was so dark I didn't see her coming.'

Beth gets up from her end of the table and removes his cap completely so she can see properly. She parts his dark hair with her fingers and touches the greyish scar the size of a twenty-cent piece.

'You go girl! She really popped you one.'

I wonder about the women who have been in his life. I remember Chloe, the girl he'd been visiting Cherbourg with when Mitchell Pringle died.

'What happened to Chloe your old girlfriend?' I ask.

'She's dead.'

I can't ask how. Already this is six deaths in our first face-to-face meeting: his mother, three brothers, his daughter, and now his girlfriend. Seven, if I count Sasha.

I need to go to the toilet so I politely ask the way and excuse myself. Errol's bathroom is clean and tidy. There's only one bar of soap and I figure he must take it backwards and forwards from sink to tub. Yellow Sunlight. There isn't another product in sight. I resist the urge to open his bathroom cabinet, as I'd do in anybody else's bathroom.

Beth and Errol have a lot of people in common. The pub Beth works in is a big Aboriginal hangout and Errol even knows members from her boyfriend's extended family.

Errol names some people he used to hang round with in Musgrave Park. Beth mentions a man who used to come in who she said was a respected Aboriginal leader.

'He's not respected!' Errol declares, outraged. 'He kicked a baby out of Yvonne.'

Eight, that's eight dead in two days.

There is nothing more to say without risking more casualties. The three of us sit tapping our cigarettes, drinking our drinks and staying quiet. Errol breaks the silence.

'When can I go see Dad?'

'Next weekend!' Beth says brightly. 'I'll take you!'

'No, not next weekend,' I say, interrupting, 'I won't be here.'

I want to be there when Errol sees Dad for the first time so I can write down my impressions. I can feel myself losing control of the situation I have created. This is my baby and I have to be there for it.

But Errol is keen.

'Can't you come back next weekend? You told me Dad is old. I don't want anything to happen to him waiting for you to come back.'

'I've got to get back to Newcastle for my job. I can organise it for maybe a month's time but not next weekend.'

'I missed seeing our Mum, and I don't want anything to happen to Dad before I have the chance to see him.'

It dawns on me, hearing him speak, what I am doing. I'm trying to control his movements for my own advantage. I've forced him into stating his losses just so he can see his own father.

'No, just ignore me,' I say, feeling sick. 'Go whenever you like.'

'If you moved back to Queensland we wouldn't have this problem.'

'Let's just say,' speaking low to cover my self-disgust, 'I'm not particularly fond of the place.'

'Little brother you listen to me. You can't be a traitor to Queensland. This is your home. You were born here.'

All these dead and he's still loyal to the place, and to me. Little brother. He called me little brother. I look down at his arm and the tattoo of Queensland. He is a true warrior and I'm a coward continually running away. If Mum was a rhino hiding behind a tree, as Beth had described her, what am I?

I know. I am the liger from Bullen's African Lion Safari. Neither here nor there.

We are at Errol's for five hours and Errol makes Beth stop drinking in the second hour because she's the one driving: 'You can't drink drive. I can't lose you now we've found each other again. I lost three brothers already like that.'

When Errol and I hug goodbye tears are running down both our cheeks. I pull out a disposable camera from the plastic bag and take photos. In the car all the way back to Beth's we roar, reliving every second.

The next day I return to Newcastle. That night I ring Errol and ask what his bank account details are so I can put money in for his son's football boots.

'No brother, no. I'm all right. I'll give him money when my payout comes through.'

'Errol, I want to – I'm his uncle and I haven't given anything to him his whole life. Think of it as a late birthday present.'

'No, that's really nice, but no.'

The List of Black Dead	*The List of White Dead*
Mitchell Pringle	*Mum*
Errol and Lindsey's Blood brother 1	*Ron*
Errol and Lindsey's Blood brother 2	*Rayley*
Errol and Lindsey's Blood brother 3	
Corey	
Sasha	
Errol's daughter	
Errol's birth mother	
Chloe	
Yvonne's baby	

New South Wales

I can't sleep with the monster storm hurling bits and pieces of Newcastle about and trying to suck the roof off. I wrap my computer, photos and decorative Aboriginal heads in plastic, just in case. Over the early morning radio comes news a ship has beached itself at Nobbys.

I cram the disposable camera containing pictures of Errol into my jacket pocket and wheel my bike through the rain to the footpath. I am about to become a part of the Newcastle tradition, stretching back past 1866 and the SS *Cawarra*, of witnessing a shipwreck in action. Tree branches litter the road. The wind viciously snatches the handlebars and turns me out onto the road. Blood. I remember my haemophiliac fantasy from childhood, and how if I were so afflicted an accident like this could spell my doom. Looming high over Hunter Street I can see a ship's bow, maroon coloured, embedded in the heart of the city like a bloody axe. It's like Queensland has come calling.

BOOM. One, two, three, BOOM. One, two, three, BOOM. Explosions reverberate over the city as one huge wave after another hits the ship.

The ship is a behemoth. I hurry past a small obelisk built to commemorate the building of the 1818 breakwall and turn down a beach track of laddered posts, taking photos of the ship the entire way. *Pasha Bulka*. I am one of the first sightseers and the only person on the sand. I race to the water's edge.

Storm clouds stride towards the city on stilts of lightning. The ship is a huge conductor. I can't die. I've just found my brother. Standing with the camera in my hand I realise the only photos on the reel will be of Errol and a shipwreck. I've turned into just another gawker, like the townspeople peering through the mist and rain while the *Cawarra* sank. But even if lives are in present danger there is nothing I can do. This maroon-coloured ship is a lesson. What was it I expected Queensland to do when my brothers were being tossed about the insides of the garage and hit with pieces of wood like flotsam during a raging storm? What did I expect Queensland to do when Ron slid silent as water over the lino of my sleeping sisters' bedrooms? Raise a muddy fist up right out of the very earth? Hurl a tree and kill him? Raise a storm to sweep him away from our mother and us? Yes, yes, yes and yes. Irrational, but yes.

*

Karen's husband arrives in Newcastle on business a few days after the storm and I take him to see the city's newest tourist attraction. The authorities have erected cyclone fencing to stop people getting too close to the ship. Apart from officials no one has access to the sand. Ryan tells me he has recently been diagnosed a type two diabetic and how after all his years of hard living he can only drink dandelion coffee. He says it with a strange vulnerability that I thought completely foreign to him.

If Lindsey and Errol were the two toughest boys southside, Ryan would have come third. I think Karen married Ryan because of his ability to protect her from any man alive. Ryan tells me he is worried about my plan to reintroduce Errol back into our lives, that Errol might have changed in unknowable ways from when we were kids. He says he is disturbed by a man who says he can't afford to buy his boy football boots. He says this isn't something you say when you first meet someone after 20 something years and adds that he thinks Errol might be after money. I gently remind Ryan that I found Errol and not the other way round, and that I have no money.

This is my doing. Me, setting people up. I started this fear rolling by telling Karen about the football boots in the first instance.

I tell Ryan I offered to buy the boots and Errol wouldn't let me.

Ryan says he is concerned, that's all.

Conveniently forgetting Ryan's diabetes we stop at the bowling club to have a few drinks. Apart from the staff we are the only ones there. The television relays the introductory interviews and panel discussions before the second game of the State of Origin series.

Shot from a helicopter, the open maw of Sydney's Telstra Stadium comes onscreen. From up high it looks like an upended turtle with its stomach eaten away. The commentators rant and rave, making much of the fact that Queensland has never won a game at Telstra Stadium. They keep referring to this phenomenon as 'a hoodoo' as if magic is involved. That Queensland is jinxed each time they run onto the turf.

'Hallelujah to that,' I mutter.

'Hey, watch it,' Ryan says.

The commentators throw statistics about like confetti. The pro-Blues commentator is gloating that the Maroons not only have to deal with the opposing players and the hoodoo, but also the hometown advantage. I doubt the power of the hometown advantage. Sydney hasn't put on much of a blue display – nothing like the ember-coloured walls of Queensland's cauldron from the first game.

In the ninth minute a Blues player scores and another converts to take the score to 6-0. Men slam into men and the commentators start pouring their usual lumpy hyperbole over the scene.

'Talk about David and Goliath,' one says gleefully.

David and Goliath. The only times I managed to hurt Ron was when I inadvertently reminded him of his own childhood abuse when I cut my foot open in the abandoned building lot, and the second time in the few hours after Mum died. And even then I couldn't do it by myself. That was a team effort.

Ryan and I were out front waiting for the undertaker. A car drove up into the cul-de-sac, and as it passed I recognised Ron's profile. He must have sensed something bad was happening. His car pulled to a stop in front of Mum's house. Ryan also recognised the driver.

'If you take one step out of that car!' Ryan yelled, stalking towards the vehicle with his raised fist, 'I'll knock your block off.'

Ron rolled the window up. *Not so tough now*, I thought.

'How's your mother?' Ron mouthed to me through the car windscreen. The look on his face was of someone incomprehensibly trapped under river ice. He even reached out his hands and pressed them flat against the windscreen.

It was entrancing.

'She's dead.' I said it triumphantly, loudly, so he had no chance of misinterpreting, and for two heartbeats nothing happened. Then his hands lost suction and floated to the sides of his head, as if moved there by invisible currents, and his body veered sideways onto the car's centre console as if in breathless, perfect agony. *Like Rasputin in the river*, I thought.

I was exhilarated. On the day my mother died.

Ron stayed bent in half, not seeing, not knowing, for an age. Then, like drowning victims everywhere, he resurfaced. Without looking at either of us he released the handbrake and the car rolled, of its own accord, down and around the corner and out of sight.

I felt as if a monster had been slain and I knew I could never have done it without Ryan. If Ryan hadn't been there Ron would have gotten out of the car and approached me and I know I would have told him gently, not because of decency, but because I would have been scared.

In the 21st minute Queensland scores and then converts to take the score to six-all.

'That Blues player should have taken the hit for the team,' Ryan exclaims, outraged. 'I'd have gotten belted instead of dumping the problem.'

I don't respond. If I were that player I would have dumped the problem as well, because now that the Queensland players have the Blues player on the ground it's like watching a pride of lions going in for the kill. The Maroon players' jaws are all working as if they've bloody flesh between their teeth. I'm a vulture – I've always known it. It's my nature. I stand back and let other men do the hard work and then I flutter down.

'NEW SOUTH WALES, NEW SOUTH WALES,' the crowd screams. In the sixty-fourth minute Queensland scores but fails to convert for two more points. The score is Maroons 10, Blues six.

The cameras capture someone in blue garb running about the perimeter of the field and zooms in. The outfit is made up of a blue body stocking and a big fake blue head decorated with a pair of yellow antennae and giant green alien eyes. I'm embarrassed to realise it's the official Blues mascot trying to rouse the crowd.

'Look at that thing!' Ryan has noticed the Blues mascot too. 'Silly as a shit beetle!'

The only reason I blame Queensland is because I'm ashamed of myself for not doing anything. Never. I stayed too scared.

The final score is 10-6. Queensland destroys the hoodoo and has now won two out of the three matches, effectively winning the Origin series.

Anastasia

Every Daffodil Day, to fight cancer, the call centre has a fund-raising morning tea on the roof in the spot usually reserved for the smokers. On Daffodil Day the smokers have to stand behind the generators. I'm the son who stood at the foot of his mother's deathbed. On Daffodil Day I wear black, sip tea and tell the story.

'Yes, she died at home in the living room with all her kids gathered round.' This is the story the call centre women want to hear and so I tell it. They're all terrified of cancer. They transpose themselves into the same place and imagine their own kids gathered about their own deathbeds.

The thing I hated most about Mum's illness was the desperate lengths she went to to stay alive. The worst was watching her try to swallow raw bone marrow from a shark, hand delivered in an ice-cream container from a fishing trawler, only to heave, and heave, and heave.

The most benign of the life-giving forces she made herself ingest was the yeast tumour wallowing in a coat of frothy bubbles also delivered in an ice-cream container. Everything vile turned up in ice-cream containers. After Mum drank the tumour's old bath water I would top up the container with cold tea. The yeast tumour lay about in the fridge doing nothing like a queen in her bath. I named her Anastasia because the yeast's forebears originated on the Russian Steppes.

I don't tell the women on the call centre roof that I was ready for my mother to die when the time finally came. I don't say I think Mum died thirsty, or recount how in her last seconds her breaths came faster and faster, like a train building up steam, or that I called out in a high, excited voice, 'Goodbye, goodbye, goodbye,' like a resident of Noddy's Toy Town waving a kerchief after a diminishing caboose.

I don't tell them how chaos ensued without our mother there as glue. How in the days after her death we pawed through her handbag and through all its zippered compartments looking for the will. How we fell upon her papers, or how quickly the house was put on the market. Or how we took loads of her stuff to the dump, where I threw her white foam head and wig away. How the head was too light and the wind kept blowing it back down the garbage pile as if it didn't want to go.

I don't tell the women on the roof that while waiting for the morticians to come, I walked to the fridge and removed Anastasia from the second shelf and dumped her in the sink. How I used a knife to cut her up and watched while pieces of her slid like junket between the tannin-stained arms of the sink grate.

*

I got the ornament of the two boys, a golden half-farthing, and one of Mum's ancestor's war medals hanging on a chain. Karen, Beth, the twins and I received the divided financial remains of our mother's estate – $20 000 each. This is the money I used to start my new life in Newcastle.

I also got an envelope with a folded letter inside, dating from the mid-eighties, explaining that at this point in time Children's Services can only give non-identifying information. I remembered Mum telling me that she had applied for this information for all of us adopted ones, but in the mid-eighties I was seeking the answers to my identity in the bars and clubs on Sydney's Oxford Street, and I don't remember hearing anything more of her enquiry.

It is recorded that David's birth mother was 30 years old and single. Her nationality was Australian and her religion was Presbyterian. She had a Scholarship education standard and was employed as a machinist. She resided in a city area. She had orange hair, green eyes and a fair complexion. She was 5ft 3 inches tall (160cm) and weighed 7st 7lb (47.8 kg). She was especially interested in sewing. No other children are recorded.

It is recorded that David's birth father was 31 years old and married. His nationality was Australian and his religion is not recorded. He had fair hair, dark blue eyes and a fair complexion. He was 6ft tall (183 cm) and described as well built. He was especially interested in riding.

David was born at 8:20pm and weighed 9lb 10ozs.

Not 13. Thirty. My birth mother was 30. And after all this time thinking my birth mother was 13. A 13 year old would really have had no choice but to give me away. Thirty is different. A 30 year old could have kept me if she tried. Even though the information is supposed to be non-identifying, the level of detail reads true: a machinist who liked sewing. I think of Anastasia for a second but it's hard to summon the Cinderella story up out of all this. Oh, the occupation is certainly Cinderella . . . ish, but Cinderella was a young woman, not a 30 year old. I'm upset at the age disparity. If my birth mother was 30 then that would make her 70 now and probably in need of care. Or perhaps she was already dead, like Mum. At least if she was 30 when she had me I'm less likely to be the outcome of a rape.

Every cloud . . .

Mum must have misheard the nurse when she transferred me to Mum's arms. Thirteen and 30 sound similar, and the guff about being very special must have been the usual midwife patter about all babies being special, even the ones given away. Thinking the information true, Mum came home from the hospital and wrote the false details in her diary, where it sat waiting for me to dig it out and believe it.

After Mum's funeral I wait a week and ring the adoption contact agency. I explain I had previously believed my birth mother was 13 when she had me, and my shock of being told she was thirty in the non-identifying information.

'It's not unheard of that the official documents were changed to protect reputations. She may well have been 13. You won't really know until you find her.'

I find the Protector of Reputations concocting 'machinist and liking sewing' hard to believe. 'Desperately beautiful, but doomed princess', is a far more realistic fantasy. No, the details of her occupation and religion are too real. Ma and Pa must have got together New Years Eve 1965, a factory machinist and a farmer out on the town having some fun, and I was born nine months later.

The woman on the phone tells me there is a register that adoptees and those who adopted them out can scan to see if their details match up, and voila, it's like a game of snap where blood matches blood. After supplying my birth date and place of birth, the woman tells me there isn't anyone who corresponds. My factory-working birth mother still doesn't want me. Too busy sewing probably. Oh well. I don't want her either.

The woman on the phone says the laws have changed since 1985 and now identifying information is available. She tells me I can now order my original birth certificate no problem.

It dawns on me that I'm selfishly mourning the idea my birth mother wasn't 13. Is that sick or what? How it had been *something* to be born by a 13 year old. But a 30-year-old woman who operated a factory sewing machine, and liked sewing, is not the story I was looking for.

When my original birth certificate arrives my birth mother's name is Frances, Frances Fisher, born in Melbourne in 1935. The space for my birth father's details are blank. The Brisbane address where Frances probably holed up while waiting to have me is also listed. A cheap boarding house, I bet. One day, I promise myself, I'll go and see where she stayed.

Family

It's pelting down when Jason and I fly into Brisbane. It's been a month since finding Errol, and luckily, for reasons unrelated to my wants, the reunion between Errol and his foster family has been postponed till this weekend. As we come in to land the airport lights have been dampened down by the rain and hang over the white terminal buildings in a beautiful golden shroud.

Beth is driving a car I don't recognise. She tells me a drunken friend confiscated her car keys the night before and then lost them. Beth is driving her boyfriend's car, which he can't drive because he lost his licence for drink driving.

'It's funny,' I tell her, 'what goes round, comes round.'

Beth takes us to an office supply shop so I can copy the photos I've brought to give Errol. The only original I plan to keep is the one of Errol, Lindsey and me on the log tower at Bullen's African Lion Safari. I remove it from the album's protective sleeve and show Beth.

'God, look at you,' she says in mock wonder. 'Why was anyone surprised?'

Before we go to bed I ring Errol to remind him of the following day's events.

'It's the family reunion this weekend remember, and I can't wait to introduce you to Jason.'

'Hey now,' he says, laughing, 'there won't be any kissing or hugging?'

'I'm sure we'll control ourselves.'

The next morning, to free up room in Beth's vehicle, Karen arrives and takes delivery of Jason so Beth and I can go and pick up Errol and her boyfriend in relative comfort.

Errol is waiting in the window when we get to his flat, but instead of coming out he calls for us to come in. There are papers spread out over the tabletop.

'Can you make any sense of these?' Errol says.

I pick up the closest sheaf and read the words.

The Redress Scheme is part of the Queensland Government's response to the recommendations of the Forde Inquiry. Under the scheme, eligible applicants receive an ex gratia payment, ranging from $7,000 up to $40,000, to acknowledge the impact of the past and help them move forward with their lives.

'God, Errol, you might get up to $40,000!'

The government acknowledges that while neglect and abuse was found to have occurred in some institutions covered by the enquiry, this was not necessarily the case with all institutions. Payment will only be made if applicants sign a Deed of Release, agreeing to make no further legal claims on the State of Queensland in relation to claims that come within the scope of the Redress Scheme.

The Redress Scheme is specific to Queensland children's institutions and does not include hospitals, adult mental health facilities, foster care or institutions specific to children with a disability.

'I can't believe the government absolved themselves of any responsibility after you were fostered,' I say, flicking through the document. 'It's their fault you were available to be fostered in the first place.'

Beth picks up another document off the table and reads out loud.

To determine whether the institution in which you were placed as a child, by the State, or by a parent or guardian, comes within the scope of the Redress Scheme, refer to the list in Appendix 1 of these guidelines.

'Nope,' she declares, theatrically, after studying the document, 'none of our old addresses are listed I'm afraid. They wipe their hands of you once they gave you to Mum and Dad.'

'So it looks like the most you can get for being taken is,' Beth states, running her finger down a page, '$7,000.'

'Na, they can forget it. What happened to me is worth more than that chicken shit.'

$7,000. I'm astounded. I think about all the money in Queensland's coffers – the money that built the cliffs of culture along the south bank of the Brisbane River, the River Walk suspended out over the water, the new bridges and the highways, the beautiful airport.

Errol locks his front door and we walk back to the car. I reach in and get my bag out of the front seat and get in the back.

'What are you doing?' he asks.

'Special guests sit in the front,' I reply, but the real truth is – I'll be able to study him better from a position in the back.

'I'm not a special guest. I'm just back from walkabout! Have you brought those photos?' he asks, turning and looking.

I hand each one through the gap and tell him he can keep them as I've made copies. The first one I pass through is of a teenage Errol opposite a small blond boy of about four, both of them concentrating on a tennis ball connected to a pole by string.

'That's Aunty Anne's son. He'll be at the reunion. Wait till you see him now.'

He calmly studies each of the images then turns his face into the breeze curling in through the open car window. From the back seat I can't work out if he's trying to remember, or trying not to.

'That's taken at Somerset Dam. You're the furthest one out on that branch over the creek in the purple shorts and blue singlet.'

'You sure that's me?'

'Positive.'

And when I say this Errol reaches his entire right arm through and grabs hold of mine. He keeps hold of my arm just looking at the image of himself as a boy standing relaxed and suspended over the rushing creek. Simultaneously letting me go and dropping the photo in his lap, Errol turns to stare out the window. This time there is no mistaking what he wants the wind to do. I wait 30 seconds for him to recover and then pass another through in an effort to make him laugh.

'Where's this photo taken?' he asks.

'Bullen's African Lion Safari.' I laugh self-consciously. 'Look at my hands.'

Errol looks at the photo of the three of us for a long time without a word.

'You're being a lion,' he says decisively.

'What?'

'You're a lion.'

'Let me see.' Stunned, I reach out my hand.

And it's true. It isn't photographic evidence of my birth as a young queen. I'm being a lion at Bullen's African Lion Safari. I've got my hands out in front of me like lion's paws and my fingers are lion claws. I'm being a lion, the king of the jungle, and my brother is the first to see it.

Beth overtakes a speeding P-plater and at the next corner the boy pulls up ready to give her a mouthful. When he sees Errol in the front seat he pulls his head in.

At the border of the Northern Suburbs and the city we stop at the lights in front of the Royal Brisbane Hospital.

'That's where I was born!' Errol points.

'That's where I was born,' I crow.

'Hey,' Beth interjects, 'I was born there too.'

'God, we're the three little pigs.'

'And Ron was the big bad wolf,' Errol says.

'Isn't it weird the thought of all our birth mothers walking the same hospital corridors?'

'Do, do, do, do. Do, do, do, do.' Beth sings the theme music from *The Twilight Zone*.

'You know, you adopted ones are also the stolen generation,' Errol states quietly.

It feels strange to hear Errol say this. It's not something I'd say myself, because colour has everything to do with being stolen. But the fact that Errol is generous enough to think this creates an overwhelming sense of rightness to the journey, that we all belong together right now.

But it's also something else. It's as if three spectral women wearing plain, cotton hospital gowns have come swooping, zooming, gliding across the road from the hospital eagerly looking into the car, reaching in their ghostly arms, stroking our hair and touching our faces, cooing, happy we remember them and happy to finally meet each other.

*

We stop to pick up Jeff and when he gets in the first thing he asks Beth is if she has lip-gloss as his lips are really dry.

'Yeah I do, in my bag,' Beth says. 'It's a bit glossy though.'

'I'm wearing it,' I say, 'and you can't tell.'

'Yeah,' Beth says, looking in the rear vision mirror, smiling, 'that's what you think.'

Jeff applies it to his lips anyway and I take this as an act that no matter what my silly sister says, he's not one to judge me.

We walk into Karen's with me leading the way. Jason, Dad, aunts, uncles, nieces and nephews, friends of the family, are all gathered waiting under the back pergola. I kiss all the women and shake all the men's hands but I'm trembling as if I'm cold, and feel desperate for a drink so I head back indoors to get a beer. On my way through I pass Beth, Jeff and Errol, who've already stopped for refreshments to steady their own nerves.

I hear Dad say 'Hello son' but I can't see him.

'I haven't seen you since you were this high.'

Everybody erupts into laughter and I can't believe I'm missing this for the sake of a drink so I rush back to the open door.

'Dad, you've got the wrong one!' Karen chimes. 'You've got hold of Jeff, Beth's boyfriend. This is Errol!'

I push through the relatives just in time to see Dad and Errol hugging and Errol giving Dad a kiss. They both look really emotional. I can't believe that, after trying to control the timing of the reunion, I nearly missed the actual meeting between them.

'This is the only Dad I had growing up,' Errol says to the gathering.

Errol stays standing behind Dad's chair for the next few hours like Dad is an old king and Errol is his warrior. People approach for an audience and I hear him answering questions about his blood family, his whereabouts all these years, his current circumstances, and whether he's seen or heard anything about Lindsey.

During a break I walk Jason over to introduce him to Errol. They shake hands but it's awkward. Our aunt is taking photos and she positions Errol alongside each of her children in turn.

'I've never been to a family reunion before,' Errol says, pretending to hoist himself up onto the shoulders of his two tall cousins.

'What about on Palm Island?' our aunt asks.

'That wasn't a reunion. I had to fight my way back in!'

Karen's husband Ryan does all the cooking and cleaning and he's not drinking. I go and stand by him and thank him for everything he's done.

'It's brilliant,' he says, 'this would never happen in my family.'

'Ryan, this is your family. You and Karen have been together for over 20 years!'

'No, you know what I mean. I don't talk to any of my brothers and sisters. When we were kids in Darwin our father used to take us on drives out into the desert and when he got bored he'd think it was fun to fire a gun at us, and we'd scatter in different directions. Mentally I don't think any of us ever came back together. I think we are too shell-shocked. You lot are all diverse and come from every which way, but you all manage to get on.'

I ask him what he thinks of Errol.

'He's cool. I was wrong.'

And I was wrong to set you up, I say to myself.

We turn and see my aunt recreating the shot of Errol playing totem tennis with her six-foot-five son.

At different times during the afternoon each of us takes time to stand silently by the rose pot where Mum's ashes are interred. Beth takes Errol to stand by it and Errol whispers something into the leaves. Dad has one beer too many, or maybe it's because of his stroke, but he has to leave early. Errol walks Dad to the car where Ryan is waiting to drive Dad home.

After Dad has left Errol returns and comments on how bad it must have been for Dad to discover Mum and us six kids gone all those years ago.

'Poor man,' Errol says, 'he didn't hit her or nothing ehh?'

'No,' I say. 'He just lied and hid his impotency from her, which is why we all ended up brothers and sisters.'

Despite his lies I'm suddenly aware I've never really considered the effect our leaving had on Dad.

Karen is getting more and more drunk and is using her karate fighting sticks in the backyard to showcase her brown belt abilities. I don't know if it's because karate is Japanese, but I hear Errol say, 'The Asians were the ones taking over and now it's the Indians you have to watch out for.' Karen says something derogatory about an

Indian taxi driver she once caught a ride with and Errol nods in agreement. I wonder how I can argue with one of this country's original inhabitants when Errol and his people fully understand the effect of people coming in and taking over.

Once the reunion is over the five of us pile into Beth's car for the drive back to her place where we are all staying the night. Beth lead-foots it because she is sick of watching everyone else on the drink.

At Beth's there aren't enough chairs in the lounge room to sit on so Beth goes into the bedroom and returns with a milk-crate and a loose cushion for the seat. It's a maroon-coloured Brisbane Broncos cushion embossed with a stylised horse head. The Broncos are Queensland's premier football team whose members make up the majority of the State of Origin squad. Beth plonks the crate down in front of Errol and tells him to sit but he just stares at the cushion in pretend awe.

'I'm not going to put my stinking arse on the Broncos,' his voice rises as if Beth has said something sacrilegious. He picks the cushion up and presses it to the side of his face. 'I'm going to use it tonight as a pillow for my head and it will give me sweet dreams!'

Beth laughs and hands out beer coolers to put our bottles in. She makes a silent show of handing me a maroon coloured one with words printed down the side.

QUEENSLAND STATE OF ORIGIN
QLD BORN
QLD BRED
WHEN I DIE, I'LL BE
QLD DEAD
ONCE A QUEENSLANDER, ALWAYS A QUEENSLANDER

'Cheers!' Everybody clinks foam-covered bottles.

I'm a Queenslander. Queensland has won two of the three games in this year's State of Origin and the third game is pointless. Queensland has won fair and square.

After another hour I need to lie down on one of the three mattresses Beth has arranged on her living room floor. Jason is already down and Jeff is asleep on the couch. Errol removes his shirt and gets ready for bed. He yawns and lowers himself down onto the last vacant mattress. Another tattoo is visible on his upper right bicep. One I haven't seen. Faded. I have to squint. I'm drunk and seeing double. The tattoo is a name, Chloe. Chloe, the name of his girlfriend he'd been with in Cherbourg the day of the fight. The girl he told me had died, but not how, or when.

'What happened to Chloe?'

'She was raped and murdered by two white men.' He rolls away smothering the tattoo. 'I was in prison and couldn't protect her.'

Beth doesn't want to sleep in her bedroom by herself, so she comes in and beds down on the floor between my mattress and Errol's, and that's how we fall asleep.

Third and final diagram of sleeping arrangements:

Hunger Strike

In the morning Errol spends a long time in the bathroom clearing his throat. He comes out and apologises for the horrible sounds, it's his bronchiolitis. I remind him how Mum used to have to hit his back to clear his lungs and how he would cough up golden orbs of phlegm. Errol says he doesn't remember. Jason leaves to spend the day with the married couple from Noosa, and Beth and Jeff leave for work. Errol and I set off to catch a river cat to the city to take up Beth's invitation of a free pub lunch. Upriver the cat glides past the migrant processing centre at Kangaroo Point.

'Look Errol,' I raise my voice over the wind, pointing at the white migrant building. 'That's the first place Mum slept in Queensland, back when she was seventeen. I bet she didn't dream the pair of us gliding past.'

'Na, she would have swum back home!'

We both laugh. I turn back to the migrant buildings and wonder which window Mum would have stood in and looked out at the brown water. The boat slides into the shadow of the Story Bridge, and the centre disappears behind the curve. I wish she had swum back home, but maybe she had been forewarned of the likes of us. She'd bought the Aboriginal heads of two boys who look like brothers before any of us had been born. She might have known what she was getting herself into. The cat slows to a stop at the Riverside Markets and we get out. Among the stalls I spot one selling chocolate croissants.

'Oh, my God, Errol look!'

'What?' He looks round like we are under imminent attack. 'What is it?'

'Chocolate kwasson!' I say it the way the French say croissant. Like a tosser. 'It's French for crescent. Do you want one?'

Errol squints at me long and hard. I can tell he's debating calling me a wanker. He doesn't.

We are *The Odd Couple* – a small, stocky Aboriginal man in shorts and thongs and a tall, white queen nibbling a chocolate croissant. It's blissful and stupid at the same time. Walking past Customs House we head towards Beth's pub.

'There used to be a park there before all that went up.' Errol indicates the phalanx of skyscrapers obscuring the view of the river from the road. 'Just above the river, that's where we used to hang out and drink. Stay on the Captain Cook Cruises.'

I remember there used to be wharves along this stretch, where cruise ships used to berth, and I imagine he means he used to creep aboard and crash out on the cushioned li-lows.

'Was it comfortable?' I ask.

'No.' He is looking at me like I've lost my mind. 'I think it would have fucking hurt!'

'I don't understand.' I realise I've missed something. 'Did you say STAY on the Captain Cook Cruises?'

'Not STAY,' he shouts like the idea is blasphemy, 'STONE. I said we used to STONE the Captain Cook Cruises as they went past.'

I spit pastry down the front of my shirt at the thought of the cruise ship passengers finding themselves under attack from stone throwing Aborigines 200 years after Cook landed.

'That's brilliant!' I say.

I can imagine the men and women sitting drinking on the river bank in the shadow of the Story Bridge being constantly reminded of their loss by the coming and going of Captain Cook. But it's not brilliant. It's futile and sad.

To change the subject I ask Errol who his best friend was in those days.

'The person with the money to buy the booze. And that would change daily.'

At the Blood and Bone Hotel, while we wait for lunch, Beth gives us complimentary money to put into the pokies. Errol sits at the first of a row of 10 differently themed machines. I sit at the second. His is called Fifty Lions and mine is The Queen of Sheba. Whenever a press of Errol's buttons achieves anything lions bolt through grass and his machine makes a galloping noise. I expect roars.

Rose petals fall in front of the Queen of Sheba's beautiful face whenever I have a successful spin but my machine stays silent. Neither of us wins anything except 10 free goes. After the money runs out the three of us go and stand in front of the photos that make up the Wall of Shame. Errol knows some of them, and Beth and Errol spend time discussing the merits of one of the Aboriginal women on show. Both agree she is really nice.

We drink beer and order steak.

*

Beth arranges a co-worker to fill in the rest of her shift, so she can spend the last few hours with us before I have to fly back to Newcastle.

'Let's go for a drive,' Beth offers cheerfully. 'Where shall we go?'

I'm turning the pages of the local newspaper and I find my glance resting on the tide times. The tide is low.

'Let's walk out to the island at Wellington Point. I'll beat you both and be crowned king.'

'What are you on about?' Errol asks.

'Don't you remember racing out to King Island?'

'Nup, I don't remember anything like that.'

I'm glad he can't remember. I'm glad he doesn't remember the two of them being held back by Ron so I could race ahead. I'm glad he can't remember that, despite my hatred of Ron, that I seized the opportunity.

The drive to Wellington Point from the city takes half an hour. Warm air peeling in the open windows rips up the vocals coming out of the radio. I can hear only fragments. We're teenagers again in a parallel universe: one where we all stayed together. Beth is laughing about something I can't make out, and Errol's fingers are tapping out a drumbeat on the window frame. Beth hits the horn and the three of us wave at a man on the street as if we recognise him, and crack up laughing when the poor bloke waves back.

Beth parks the car and we go to the kiosk and buy some hot chips for the walk to the island. The sand pathway isn't as red as I remember.

'What do you reckon the island was called by the local Aborigines before whites came?' Beth says, shielding her eyes with her hand.

'Dunno,' Errol shrugs.

'I bet it was called Turtle Island!' Beth says, outlining the island with her finger. 'See how it's shaped like a sea turtle pulling itself up on to the sand to lay its eggs?'

'You might be right sister girl,' Errol says, generously slinging his arm round her shoulders, 'you might have some Aborigine in you!'

'My original birth records say I was Indian,' Beth says shyly, 'but I know sometimes that was code for Aboriginal.'

'Before whites came I bet this island was really significant,' I say, trying to join in.

'It was all significant,' Errol states grimly, turning his head and taking it all in. 'We didn't carve little slices off here and there and turn them into national parks.'

'Good try David!' Beth laughs and holds her hand out for me to take.

And it is in this fashion that the three of us, Beth in the middle and Errol with his arm along her shoulders, prepare to take our first simultaneous step onto King Island. At the last second I bend down on the pretence of dislodging a stone from my shoe. Errol keeps walking and is first on the island. I mouth the words *YOU ARE KING,* still bowing, without either of them seeing.

*

That afternoon Jason and I pack our bags in preparation for our flight back to Newcastle. Errol says he feels sad. I do too.

'I love you!' he yells out, as the cab pulls away from the kerb, loud enough for the entire street to hear.

*

Member number 1696703

Cora Morgan born 14/03/1932, rings to confirm whether she has cover for major eye surgery as she needs an operation for a degenerative eye disorder. Even without the medical item number I know she isn't covered. Cora Morgan has been a member for over 20 years and used to have top cover but changed to a lower level five years ago when her husband died. I say it's a pity she hadn't stayed on her old cover.

'My husband needed that cover but I didn't,' she says. 'He became very sick after our son went missing 18 years ago.'

She didn't say murdered or killed, she said missing.

I look round to check my supervisor isn't listening. I drop my voice.

'Did you ever find your son?'

'No.'

'Was he depressed?'

'Yes. He'd only been married for 14 months before he went missing and I need this operation in case he comes back. I have to be able to see him. I keep my hairstyle the same. I try to look the same, but I'm all changing. I'm so old now I wonder if he'll recognise me.'

'Sons don't forget what their mothers look like,' I say.

'He was a lovely boy with a good sense of humour,' she says, ignoring my solemn tone. 'He used to tell me that when I got too old, he wouldn't put me into an old people's home, but would tie me up with rope and leave me under a big tree. I'm waiting for him. I've grown a big tree in the backyard.'

To prove it's not impossible, and that she's not the only one,

I tell her I found my missing brother who ran away in 1980. She gasps and adds up my brother's missing years.

'That's 27 years!' she proclaims. 'That's wonderful. That's truly wonderful. Why did he run away?'

I tell her about our stepfather.

'You've given me hope. What's your name so I can let you know if I find my son?'

I give my name and the call centre operating hours and tell her to ring after seven so she won't get stuck in a queue. Before the call ends I repeat that she isn't covered for major eye surgery and she'll have a one-year waiting period if she changes, but she doesn't seem to mind. I remember how as a kid I wanted to be a doctor or a nurse and all I managed was to get a job in a telephone call centre selling health insurance, but now that doesn't feel so bad.

During my tea break I ring Errol's mobile number and when he answers I can hear him surrounded by the whir of a Queensland electric train.

'Where are you going?'

'To Beth's place to watch the final State of Origin, and to pick up some weed. I finally got my payout.'

'I thought you said you stopped smoking!'

'Don't worry about me brother. I'm not getting back into it. I might buy myself an ounce and just have some on weekends.'

'Buying an ounce sounds like getting back into it!' I scold. 'You'd stopped for two years.'

'I just bought a new pair of shoes,' Errol says, politely changing the subject, 'guess how much!'

'Oh, I don't know.'

'$240.'

'Oh, Errol, don't waste your money.'

'They're for my son.'

'Oh, that's great.' *Just ignore me. This is none of my business.* 'Where abouts are you now? Which suburb?'

'The train is just pulling out of Brunswick Street. I'm getting off at Central and then I'll get on one going to Cleveland.'

We say our goodbyes and I hang up.

For the first time in decades I know exactly where he is. He's on a train heading towards Central, and then he'll get on another train heading to Beth's. I know exactly where he'll be for at least the next four hours and this fact gives me a perverse joy.

When I arrive home from work I ring Beth. Her phone is engaged. I try again later and she is pissed and unable to speak coherently. Errol has gone home. Beth tells me she isn't going to help Errol get the ounce he wants, that she only gave him a little bit for his sore back. Then she states she shouldn't have to feel responsible for a grown man. That her only responsibility is towards herself.

'Go the Maroons!' she yells in parting.

I turn on the television news and the score for the final State of Origin is Queensland 18 and New South Wales 4. The series has been a whitewash. Queensland won every game.

*

I'm a search junkie and I know I've got a problem when, between genuine health insurance enquiries, I start cold calling all the F. Fishers listed in the electronic phone directory. If an old woman answers I frantically whisper I'm adopted and looking for my birth mother who gave birth to me in 1965. This approach isn't the way the support agencies like it to be done. Apparently calls from out of the blue, out of the mouths of their abandoned babes, terrify the birth parent. Nine times out of 10 they hang up in a panic, and then they get silent numbers, but I don't care. Part of me enjoys the thought of scaring her.

*

A psychic woman on television strokes a child's shoe. Children's names and ages swim up out of the depths of the television screen.

Jane 9, Arnna 7, Grant 4.

The Beaumont children. Following a lead the investigators dig up a cement floor but find nothing. I wonder if instead of being dead the three children were brainwashed and raised in another family somewhere else. But then I think this wouldn't have been possible. Somebody would have noticed three kids just turning up out of nowhere and alerted the authorities. But then I think of Lindsey and Errol, and how the only question people ever asked mum about their point of origin was, 'Where did you get them?' – as if they were shop-bought.

Back in Brisbane, after a quick flight, I buy a bottle of red wine to visit Errol. I haven't told him I'm coming, but my plan is to read Errol what I've written and to ask him if the bits I've taken from his life are okay to use. I catch the train and walk the several blocks to his street. Errol already has a visitor. A white man, my age, my height, work stained fingers, dusty jeans and boots, sitting at his table. Errol introduces me to Ross and says they used to work together in the same factory. Ross is fiddling with a small magnifying glass attached to his key ring and doesn't look up as Errol explains their relationship. Errol tells Ross that I'm his foster brother and gets up and retrieves the clump of family photos I'd delivered to him on the previous visit. Errol extracts the picture taken at Bullen's African Lion Safari and points out Lindsey. Then he points me out.

'He's being a lion,' Errol makes a paw brimming with claws with his hand 'see, with his hands.'

Ross grunts. I'm intruding on Ross's real reason for being here and I suddenly feel possessive.

What do you want from my brother, white man?

I want this man to prove his credentials. Ross casually pulls a photo from the pile and I recognise the picture of Mum sitting at her kitchen table wearing the wig donated by the Cancer Council. The look on my mother's face is of real pain. Pain at everything. I don't know why I took the photo.

Ross looks closely at our mother through his magnifying glass. He fails to make the appropriate sounds about loss people would normally make. He moves the focus of the magnifying glass to an area over our mother's head. He busies himself deciphering the labels on the cans and bottles that sit on the open kitchen shelves behind her. He ignores the pain of my mother. He calls out the brand names of the products Mum has in her cupboard and makes disparaging remarks about some of them. I want him to stop, but it's not my house, he's not my guest, and it's not my photo. Errol is smiling indulgently, unaware this autopsy of our mother's kitchen, a kitchen Errol never ate in, is a knife in my gut.

Part of me wishes I'd thought to look at the same photo with a magnifying glass. To enlarge the image and make it seem like I'm back there so I can tell her how beautiful she is without the wig. I want to snatch the photo – I don't want this man looking at my mother's things like he's casing the joint. I hate this man, and then it dawns on me. This man is a junkie and he's after Errol's money.

The irony sinks in.

This man is my doppelganger. He has come on the same day to ask for Errol's money as I have come to ask for Errol's stories. The timing can't be a coincidence. I imagine it to be the work of ghosts, Errol's mothers, my mother, maybe even my birth mother setting this up, sending me a lesson to tell me they are watching what I'll do with all our stories.

Even though the sound is turned down Errol's focus is on Barack Obama on the television. Ross lifts his head from the photo to see what's captured Errol's attention.

'There won't be a black American President in this generation,' Ross says definitely.

Errol doesn't respond and just keeps watching.

Don't be so sure,' I exclaim, shocked he can be so certain, shocked he would say such a thing in front of my brother. 'Look at Condoleezza Rice, Americans like her. And who is that African American bloke who retired?'

'Colin Powell,' Errol says without thinking.

'Yeah him,' I say, wondering just how bad Errol's memory is. 'Americans liked him too.'

When Ross sees me refilling my glass, he pushes back his chair and rises from the table.

Ross looks to be going.

Yay, I think. *I've won.*

'Adios Amigos, I gotta go see my old woman.'

'Yeah, see ya brother,' Errol says, without any irony. 'Look after yourself.'

I wait until the door clicks shut.

'Who was that guy?' I ask, like I've a right to know. 'He looks dodgy.'

'I told him I was getting a payout and ever since then he keeps coming round to borrow money.' Errol chuckles, shaking his head. 'You turning up ruined his chance.'

'I hope you haven't given him any.'

'I've lent him some but I'm not giving him any more until he pays the first lot back.'

The idea of reading my work out to Errol is now too awful to contemplate.

Feeling ill I also get up to leave. I apologise for dropping in unannounced.

'Hey don't worry about it. That's what family does.'

Walking back to the train station I don't know who I am. What really cracks me up is realising, now I've found him, that Errol calls everyone brother.

*

At the State library, I load the microfilm reel of Queensland newspapers to try and locate the article about Lindsey's arrest for attempted blackmail of homosexuals in city parks. I start the slow acceleration and deceleration through Australia's recent history. Like children going on a car trip the three little Beaumont faces slide by. That's twice in one day. I wonder if the Beaumonts are an omen, or whether I'm just caught in the spokes of the cycle where every few years there's a revival of interest in what might have happened to them.

I decide this will be my last documented account of my search for Lindsey. It's not acceptable for me to write about him if he's confined to a mental hospital, and if I'm faithful to the truth, I know I don't want to find him. I'm scared that if I don't like what I find I'll retreat, and I wonder what this retreat will look like: after how many visits to the hospital? One? Two? Three? Will I have to sign him out to take him for walks? On the final walk will I tell him I'm not coming back? Will I tell him I only looked for him because I knew if I found one without the other my concept of brotherhood is flawed.

It's while I'm thinking all of this, and scrolling half-heartedly at the same time, that my vision snags on the word Aboriginal.

Aboriginal Woman bashed to death, court told.

Sasha Rebato, 27, of West End, was found dead in her bed at the Musgrave Hostel early on May 7, Brisbane Magistrates Court was told. Police charged Rhonda Pringle, 25, of West End, with Sasha Rebato's murder after Rebato was found with multiple bruises to the head and neck. Police alleged Pringle bashed Rebato after finding her in bed with Pringle's de facto husband. Rebato suffered a brain hemorrhage and injuries consistent with punching and kicking, the court was told. Forensic pathologist David Williams, who examined Sasha Rebato's body, said her injuries were caused by severe force and not a simple fall. Mr. Williams said Rebato had brain shrinkage from chronic alcoholism, which made her prone to subdural hematoma – bleeding between the brain and its surrounding membrane caused by head trauma. Mr. Williams said Rebato had suffered a previous brain hemorrhage and there was 'always a risk of re-bleed'. The hearing will continue today.

Sasha, the hungry little girl in the lilac dress, died a violent death. There's no room to wish things had turned out differently. If Mum had been successful in her wish to keep Lindsey, Errol and Sasha together, then Ron would have done to her what he did to Rayley, and Rayley's dead as well. Wishing the three of them were never stolen is as pointless as throwing stones at Captain Cook Cruises. Sasha went on a hunger strike. For Sasha, finding two brothers after going hungry for so long, must have been like a gift from God.

Compared to Sasha and what she did as a sister, I'm a nothing brother who can't stop moaning *woe is me, Queensland did me wrong*. Suddenly my thoughts crystallise into words I didn't think possible, and I cover my mouth to stop them.

'I'm not their brother.'

I'm not their brother, foster or otherwise, and with Lindsey, I admit, I've known it all along. His mental illness scares me. Brother is just a word, because there isn't any other to describe these relationships.

I know from Lindsey's one surviving memory of childhood pre-removal that the government stalked them like lions in long grass till they were the right age to be taken. I know this from published reports and watching TV, but still I've never questioned my own position within this framework.

If you knowingly receive stolen goods you are guilty. Mum knew what the government was doing was wrong, she told me. The literal version of brother I've been using is from the instruction manual for thieves who want to forget they are thieves.

Sasha went on a hunger strike. I went online and ate my chocolate croissant away from the computer so I wouldn't get crumbs in the keys.

This surely must be one of those moments alluded to on the printed card at work back in Newcastle: 'Life is not measured by the number of breaths we take, but by the moments that take our breath away.'

I am exhausted and empty.

My eyes rest on the murderer's surname.

Pringle. That name rings a bell.

And then it comes: the awful symmetry. Pringle is the last name of the young bloke who committed suicide in the Cherbourg watch-house. If Rhonda Pringle is related to Mitchell Pringle she is also related to Errol's ex-girlfriend Chloe, the girl raped and murdered by two whites.

Errol said the community blamed him for Mitchell's death. I wonder whether revenge for Mitchell had anything to do with Rhonda's rage, or whether it's because this community is so intertwined that if you're going to murder someone, invariably it's someone connected to you.

I scroll back to the beginning of the newspaper reel, past the Beaumont children on their interminable journey through the nation's consciousness and place the microfilm spool on the return tray. Mum always told us to remember the Beaumont children and I remember them now. They're the last nail in the coffin. If the Beaumont children were kidnapped off the street and forced to live in a house with other children, the other children wouldn't automatically become their brothers and sisters.

*

Walking back into the city over the Victoria Bridge I can't stop my face crumpling up like rubbish. There must be a way I can salvage my family. Maybe I should return to the library, find a dictionary, and look up the word brother.

YOU SHOULDN'T NEED A DICTIONARY TO WORK OUT WHAT BROTHER MEANS.

I realise from the shifting faces of my fellow pedestrians that I'm yelling. I don't care.

I stop against the bridge railing and summon up a collection of the world's most famous brothers:

- Cain and Abel
- Romulus and Remus
- The Brothers Grimm
- Peter and Tim Costello.

I laugh a hopeless sound. The other pedestrians give me as wide a berth as possible. At least laughing loosens my facial muscles. Tim Costello is a decent man who does a lot of work for victims of the tsunami but this list is ridiculous, and to compound the problem, each set I've come up with, except for the Brothers Grimm, is of the same blood.

I need to ring home.

'Jason, tell me quickly all the sets of brothers in the world you can think of.'

'What's wrong?'

'I need a list of brothers like Cain and Abel.'

'Jeez, nothing biblical. How about The Bee Gees . . . ' He thinks for a bit. 'Or the Baldwin brothers. Will that do?'

'No,' I say.

'You sound terrible. You need to come home.'

'I can't. Not yet. I love you. Talk later.'

There is no example for me to follow. My relationship with Lindsey and Errol can't come from outside, it has to come from within, like it has all along.

Errol did say when I found him, *my foster brother, David?*

Errol said I could drop in anytime because that's what family does.

Errol's not questioning whether our relationship is correct or not.

Foster brother is Errol's title for me. This title is good enough for him. Surely if I'm to be disowned it has to come from Errol and not the other way round. Even if we both know his forced removal was stealing. And we both do.

I try to smile a smile not too shy and not a grin.

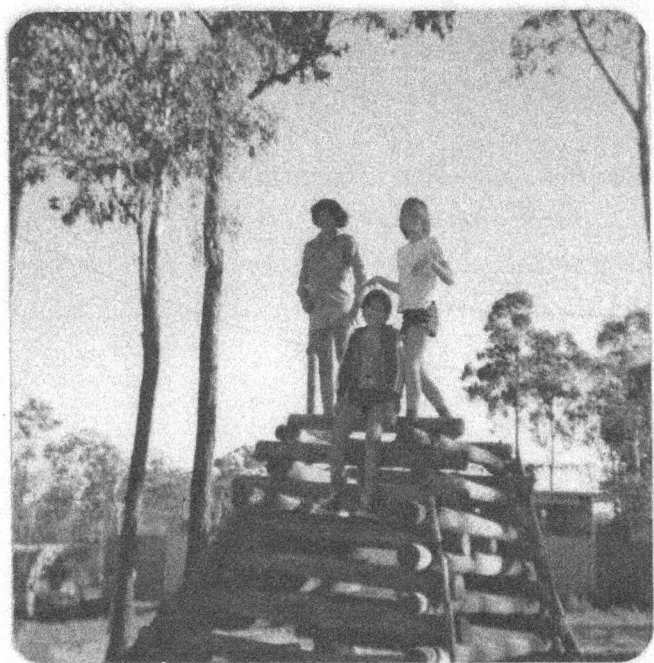

Final Tally

The white deaths are paltry in comparison. I cast my mind over the back catalogue of white faces who've played a part in this story and remember that poor Brian who'd been with me the night I met Jason died of a heroin overdose in London. I add his name to the list.

The List of Black Dead	The List of White Dead
Mitchell Pringle	*Mum*
Blood brother 1	*Ron*
Blood brother 2	*Rayley*
Blood brother 3	*Brian*
Corey	
Sasha	
Errol's daughter	
Errol's birth mother	
Chloe	
Yvonne's baby	

Ornament

The address on my original birth certificate showing where Frances stayed during her pregnancy is now a family home behind a high wooden fence with a security keypad for entry. I'm reminded of 'The House of Special Purpose' in Ekaterinburg where the Romanovs were murdered, except this house in Red Hill is about life. There were a lot of 'Houses of Special Purpose' in cities of Australia back in the day. Houses where women travelled from interstate to give birth in secret and save their family from shame – before returning home, empty-handed.

My birth mother would have caught the train up from Melbourne with a suitcase or two before her bump became too noticeable. She would have disembarked at South Brisbane train station and caught a tram or taxi across the Brisbane River to this house.

A plastic slippery slide sits protected from the weather on the verandah. The current occupants must have a child, or children. Despite the keypad and the fresh paint job, I can imagine how the outside of the place would have looked in 1965. Red corrugated iron roof, coloured glass panes in the upper window panels, chipped and faded house paint. Trams trundling along the street in front.

Frances may have even worn a pawnbroker wedding ring so she could move round undetected in the months she planned to be in Brisbane. She may have gone on little day trips. She may have gone to the Brisbane EKKA. She may even have visited the museum and stood in front of Mrs Watson's tank and seen similarities in their conditions: two women frightened away from their homes with no idea what would happen to their babies.

I press the buzzer. Through the gap between the house and the neighbours I can see the olive green slump of Mt Coot-tha wearing its television towers like party hats.

This is a good omen. There's a small wish inside me that my birth mother herself will open the front door and come to the fence. That she stayed in Brisbane all this time and bought the house in the hope I would one day turn up.

A man comes out with a small boy trotting by his side. In a voice halting with emotion I introduce myself and show him, through the fence, where his home address is listed on my original birth certificate. I'm a door-to-door salesman selling myself instead of vacuum cleaners. I tell the owner I'm researching my origins. He nods at my story and says that in the early sixties the house had been divided into six flats. I ask him if I could come in and see the view from the back landing. My request sounds whiney. He says so much work has been done on the house that the house and its interior have no relevance to this story of mine. I say it would only take a minute. No relevance he repeats.

For a split second I imagine kicking down the gate. *How dare you tell me what's relevant.*

I ask if this is his final decision.

The man nods and repeats his claim there is no relevance. In a fog of confusion I thank him for his time and move away. I want to yell, 'I was a foetus in that house!'

I didn't think rejection would affect me in this way, but then I didn't think I was going to be rejected.

Moving slowly back along the street I wonder what the homeowner would say if I went back and asked if there might be other reasons for his refusal. Maybe he would say I'm too old to be looking for my mother, or that I'm scary. Or maybe he would say he's sick of his house being a pilgrimage site for middle-aged adoptees tramping up from the city. I want to turn back and yell something about him selling renovation wood chips outside his security fence as relics. Tell him I'd buy a piece.

But yelling on the street would be scary.

I feel insulted and chastised and I start to wonder if the homeowner is right.

In comparing my reasons for searching I know my whole heart was implicated with finding Errol, but only a quarter of it with Frances.

Deep down I wonder if my reaction to the homeowner's rejection is about being denied, not my birth mother, but access to more opportunities and settings where I could elaborate on my fantasies: I'm addicted to make-believe. Filling the empty air with an actual someone would have removed so many possibilities. I'd have had to deal with real flesh and blood.

On the flipside, I'm going to ask Errol if he wants the ornament of the plaster of Paris boys. This ornament has represented my foster brothers for far too long. He can throw it in the river if he wants to.

And there's another thing: I started this search wondering what 'brother' means – and what right I have to use that term with Errol: Errol my Indigenous foster brother who hasn't the option of developing a relationship with his real mother, for she is dead.

If I forego searching for my birth mother I can be even more level with him, and maybe just a touch more real. Maintaining this absence in my own life is the only thing of substance I can give him, and show I'm more than just words.

*

Trudging back into the city I remember our long-ago, mythical, backyard. Lindsey in the loquat, armed to the teeth waiting to repel any invasion. Errol in his corner privet, surrounded by tiny birds called Silvereye. I see myself in my privet's highest branches. *Where are my sisters?* I want to play the Romanovs one last time. There they are! Even though they were never at this house the twins are lying on a blanket beneath the clothesline waving their tiny fists like pale tendrils. Karen and Beth are laughing, chasing one another around the umbrella and the coffee trees, and there beneath the hanging yellow fruit of the lemon I see Rayley and Sasha, almost invisible, together in the shadows. They are taking it in turns playing Brown Snake and Hunger Strike.

I call, but they're so obsessed, they don't hear me.

THE END

Acknowledgements

I acknowledge the Jagera, Yuggera, and Ugarapul people, the traditional custodians of my story's birthplace. *State of Origin* was written as part of a Ph.D. at the University of Newcastle with the support of an APA Scholarship. I want to thank my supervisors Brooke Collins-Gearing and Keri Glastonbury, and Scott Brewer for early editing. I thank my family for the grace they display when I rake over family coals. (Most names have been changed as a matter of course.) I thank my friends for their love and kindness, Ed Wright and David Musgrave at Puncher and Wattmann for saying yes, and Ed for editing and bringing it to publication.

David Owen Kelly is the author of *Fantastic Street*, and other bits and pieces. He lives in Newcastle.

www.ingramcontent.com/pod-product-compliance
Lightning Source LLC
Chambersburg PA
CBHW020905100426
42737CB00044B/384